Turkish

This edition published in 2010
LOVE FOOD is an imprint of Parragon Books Ltd

Parragon
Queen Street House
4 Queen Street
Bath BA1 1HE, UK

ISBN: 978-1-4454-2057-8

Printed in China

Designed by Terry Jeavons & Company

This book uses both metric and imperial measurements. Follow the same units of measurement throughout; do not mix metric and imperial. All spoon measurements are level: teaspoons are assumed to be 5 ml, and tablespoons are assumed to be 15 ml. Unless otherwise stated, milk is assumed to be full fat, eggs and individual vegetables are medium, and pepper is freshly ground black pepper.

The times given are an approximate guide only. Preparation times differ according to the techniques used by different people and the cooking times may also vary from those given. Optional ingredients, variations or serving suggestions have not been included in the calculations.

Recipes using raw or very lightly cooked eggs should be avoided by infants, the elderly, pregnant women, convalescents and anyone suffering from an illness. Pregnant and breastfeeding women are advised to avoid eating peanuts and peanut products. Sufferers from nut allergies should be aware that some of the ready-made ingredients used in the recipes in this book may contain nuts. Always check the packaging before use.

Vegetarians should be aware that some of the ready-made ingredients used in the recipes in this book may contain animal products. Always check the packaging before use.

Turkish

introduction

The cuisine of Turkey has an intriguing mix of influences taken both from its own history and from its position. The country borders several Middle Eastern countries and its culinary repertoire shares many of their traditional dishes, or variations of them. However, it is also one of the many countries that border the Mediterranean Sea, and thus there are certain elements of the uncomplicated, health-enhancing Mediterranean diet to be found, too. The result of this blend of Eastern and Western traditions is quite simply delicious.

Turkish food is spicy but not fiery, the flavours coming mainly from pepper, paprika, cinnamon and allspice. Herbs are also used

subtly, the most popular being parsley, mint, dill and bay leaves. If possible, grow at least some parsley and mint at home, even if only in a pot on a sunny windowsill – the fresh taste and vibrant colour are well worth the effort.

Rice is an essential ingredient in Turkish cookery. A simple pilaf of white rice cooked in chicken stock is the favourite accompaniment for many dishes, or the rice can be spiced or vegetables added for flavour and colour.

The most popular meat is lamb, but beef is also used and many recipes, especially minced-meat kebabs and stuffed vegetables, work equally well using either lamb or beef. Chicken is another popular option, often simply grilled or barbecued or added to a pilaf, although a special-occasion dish is Circassian chicken, served with a walnut sauce and drizzled with paprika steeped in walnut oil.

Vegetables form a very important part of the diet and include

aubergines, peppers and tomatoes, all of which are served stuffed, as well as spinach, chickpeas and okra, a curiously textured fibrous pod commonly known as 'ladies' fingers'.

This book has a wonderful selection of typical Turkish dishes to try, so get cooking and enjoy a new experience!

meze
& soups

One of the great joys of eating in the Turkish style is the 'meze' – a collection of appetizers to be lingered over at the start of a meal. Perhaps the best-known of these is the stuffed, braised aubergine dish known as Imam Biyaldi, which translates, delightfully, to 'the priest swooned', although it is not quite clear whether he swooned because the dish was so delicious or his wife overspent on the household budget! Stuffed Courgettes, Artichokes with Broad Beans and Stuffed Vine Leaves are equally good to eat, although these dishes lack such a descriptive name.

Dips are a favourite element of meze, and in this chapter you will find recipes for an Aubergine Dip with a fresh lemon flavour, as well as the chickpea dip – Hummus – served in many regions in the country, and Cod Roe dip. Freshly baked Turkish Pide, or pocket bread, is the perfect partner for dips, and is so easy to make – try the recipe on page 164.

Soups are very popular in Turkey and are often thickened with a distinctive egg yolk and lemon mixture. Wedding Soup is traditionally served just after the ceremony, but it's a hearty, warming soup for a chilly non-festive day, too! In very hot weather, nothing is more refreshing than Cold Cucumber Soup, served with an ice cube or two and garnished with a sprig of fresh mint.

imam biyaldi

ingredients

SERVES 4

4 large aubergines, stalks
    removed
sea salt
150 ml/5 fl oz olive oil
about 4 tbsp water
2 tbsp lemon juice
1 tsp sugar or honey

filling

2 tbsp olive oil
2 onions, thinly sliced
2 garlic cloves, peeled and
    finely chopped
4 large tomatoes, peeled,
    deseeded and chopped
½ tsp ground allspice
large bunch of fresh flat-leaf
    parsley, chopped
salt and pepper

method

1 Make 3 incisions lengthways in the aubergines, taking care not to cut all the way through. Place the aubergines in a colander, sprinkle with salt, place a plate on top and place a weight on the plate. Drain for 1 hour.

2 To make the filling, heat the olive oil in a saucepan over medium heat, add the onions and cook, stirring occasionally, for about 5 minutes, or until softened but not browned. Add the garlic and cook, stirring, for a further minute. Remove from the heat and stir in the tomatoes, allspice and parsley. Season to taste with salt and pepper and cool a little.

3 Rinse the aubergines under cold running water and pat dry with kitchen paper. Spoon the filling into the incisions in the aubergines and arrange the stuffed aubergines in the bottom of a large saucepan.

4 Mix the 150 ml/5 fl oz of olive oil together with 4 tablespoons of water, the lemon juice and sugar or honey. Pour the mixture around the aubergines, then cover the pan and cook the aubergines over low heat for 45–60 minutes, or until tender. Add a little extra water only if necessary.

5 Remove from the heat and cool in the pan to room temperature. Transfer to a serving dish and serve cold.

aubergine slices stuffed with cheese

ingredients

SERVES 8

2 large aubergines

salt

3–4 tbsp olive oil, plus extra
    for deep frying

225 g/8 oz cream cheese or
    grated Provolone cheese

3 eggs

3 tbsp finely chopped fresh
    flat-leaf parsley

115 g/4 oz fine dry
    breadcrumbs

sprig of fresh flat-leaf parsley,
    to garnish

method

1 Slice the aubergines lengthways, then cut each slice into 3 rectangles. Place the slices in a colander, sprinkle with a little salt and drain for 30 minutes. Rinse under cold running water and pat dry with kitchen paper.

2 Heat the olive oil in a heavy-based frying pan and fry the aubergine slices, in batches, until soft and lightly coloured, adding a little more oil between batches if necessary. Remove from the pan and drain on kitchen paper.

3 Beat the cream cheese with a fork. Beat 2 of the eggs and add them, with the parsley, to the cream cheese. Mix thoroughly, then spread a little of the mixture over half of the aubergine slices. Top with the remaining slices and press lightly.

4 Beat the remaining egg in a shallow dish and spread out the breadcrumbs in another shallow dish. Dip the aubergine slices into the beaten egg, then coat with breadcrumbs.

5 Heat the oil for deep-frying in a deep, heavy-based frying pan until a cube of day-old bread browns in 30 seconds. Fry the aubergine slices, in batches, for 2–3 minutes, until golden brown. Remove from the pan and drain thoroughly on kitchen paper. Serve hot, garnished with parsley.

aubergine dip

ingredients

SERVES 4

2 aubergines

3 tbsp olive oil

3 tbsp chopped fresh flat-leaf
    parsley

2 garlic cloves, crushed

juice of 1 lemon

salt and pepper

warm pitta bread, to serve

method

1 Rinse the aubergines, pat them dry and place them under a grill preheated to the highest setting. Grill the aubergines, turning frequently, until the skins are black and starting to blister and the flesh has softened. Rub the skins off under cold running water, then gently squeeze out as much of the juice as possible.

2 Place the aubergines in a food processor and process until smooth. Alternatively, place them in a bowl and mash them with a fork. Add the oil gradually, then add most of the chopped parsley, the garlic, lemon juice and salt and pepper to taste. Mix thoroughly. Taste and adjust the seasoning, if necessary.

3 Sprinkle with the remaining chopped parsley and serve with warm pitta bread.

stuffed courgettes

ingredients

SERVES 4–6

900 g/2 lb courgettes, stems
    removed
2 tomatoes, sliced
about 150 ml/5 fl oz olive oil
300 ml/10 fl oz water
1 tsp sugar
salt

filling

350 g/12 oz onions, very
    finely sliced
3 tbsp olive oil
2 large garlic cloves, crushed
large bunch of fresh flat-leaf
    parsley, finely chopped
350 g/12 oz tomatoes,
    deseeded and chopped
salt

method

1 Wash the courgettes, sprinkle with salt and drain for 30 minutes to soften them.

2 Meanwhile, prepare the filling. Slice the onions thinly. Heat the olive oil in a large, heavy-based frying pan over medium–low heat and cook the onions until soft but not browned. Add the garlic and stir for a further minute. Remove the pan from the heat and stir in the parsley and tomatoes. Season to taste with salt and mix well.

3 Using an apple corer, make a hole at the stem end of each courgette and very carefully scoop out the pulp, being careful not to pierce the skin. Stuff the courgettes with the onion and tomato mixture.

4 Arrange the sliced tomatoes in the bottom of a large saucepan and arrange the courgettes on top. Mix the olive oil with 300 ml/10 fl oz of water, the sugar and a little salt. Cover the pan tightly and simmer gently over low heat for about $1\frac{1}{2}$ hours, or until the courgettes are soft. Serve at room temperature.

courgette fritters

ingredients

SERVES 4

450 g/1 lb courgettes

1 tsp salt

8 tbsp chopped spring onions
(green part only)

1 small onion, grated

8 tbsp chopped fresh dill

4 tbsp chopped fresh flat-leaf
parsley

115 g/4 oz feta cheese,
crumbled

4 eggs, lightly beaten

150 g/5 oz plain flour

salt and pepper

olive oil

method

1 Grate the courgettes into a colander, sprinkle with salt and drain for 30 minutes, then squeeze out the moisture and pat dry with kitchen paper.

2 Place the courgettes in a bowl, add the spring onions, onion, dill, parsley, feta cheese, eggs and flour and season to taste with salt and pepper. Stir to mix thoroughly.

3 Heat some olive oil to a depth of $1/2$ cm/$1/4$ inch in a large frying pan over medium–high heat. Drop generous tablespoons of the courgette mixture into the hot oil, in batches to avoid overcrowding, and cook for 5–6 minutes, turning once, until crisp and golden brown. Remove from the pan and drain thoroughly on kitchen paper. Serve hot.

artichokes with broad beans

ingredients

SERVES 4

4 tbsp lemon juice

4 globe artichokes

125 ml/4 fl oz olive oil

2 large onions

250 g/9 oz broad beans,
    shelled

225 ml/8 fl oz water

1 tsp salt

3 tbsp chopped fresh dill

method

1 Fill a large bowl with cold water and add the lemon juice. Snap the stem off one artichoke, then peel away the tough outer leaves. Snip or break off the tough tops of the remaining leaves. Cut off the top 2 cm/¾ inch of the central cone with a sharp knife. Drop the artichoke into the bowl of water and prepare the others.

2 Heat the olive oil in a saucepan large enough to hold the artichokes in a single layer. Cook the onions for about 5 minutes, or until softened but not browned. Drain the artichokes and add them to the pan with the broad beans, water and salt. Bring to the boil over low heat, cover the pan and simmer for 15 minutes, or until the artichokes and beans are nearly tender. Stir in the chopped dill and cook for a further 5–10 minutes, or until the artichokes and beans are tender.

3 Remove the artichokes from the pan, drain well and set aside until cool enough to handle. Gently separate the leaves, then remove the central cones with a teaspoon and discard. Arrange the artichokes on a serving plate and fill with the broad bean mixture. Serve at room temperature.

stuffed vine leaves

ingredients

SERVES 4

225 g/8 oz preserved vine
  leaves, drained
150 ml/5 fl oz olive oil
150 ml/5 fl oz water
juice of 1 lemon
1 tsp sugar

filling

225 g/8 oz long-grain rice
40 g/1½ oz pine nuts
4 tbsp spring onions, finely
  chopped
2 tbsp finely chopped fresh
  flat-leaf parsley
2 tbsp dried mint
½ tsp ground cinnamon
½ tsp ground allspice
salt and pepper

method

1 Place the vine leaves in a large bowl and cover with boiling water. Soak for 20 minutes, then drain. Soak for a further 2 minutes in fresh cold water and drain again.

2 Place the rice in a bowl, cover with boiling water, stir and let stand for 5 minutes. Transfer to a sieve and rinse under cold running water. Drain well.

3 Mix the rice with the pine nuts, spring onions, parsley, mint, cinnamon and allspice and season to taste with salt and pepper.

4 Place one vine leaf on a cutting board, vein side up. Place a heaped teaspoon of the filling in the centre of the leaf near the stem. Fold the stem over the filling, then fold in the sides and roll into a neat package. Continue until all the whole leaves have been used up, setting aside any torn leaves.

5 Line the bottom of a large, heavy-based saucepan with the reserved torn leaves and arrange the stuffed leaves on top. Mix the olive oil with the water, lemon juice and sugar and pour over the stuffed leaves. Place a plate on top to keep the rolls in shape.

6 Place the pan over medium heat and bring to the boil. Reduce the heat, cover the pan and simmer gently for 1½ hours, or until the rolls are cooked. Remove from the heat and cool to room temperature before serving.

white bean salad

ingredients

SERVES 6

400 g/14 oz dried cannellini
　beans, soaked overnight in
　cold water and drained

salt

1 garlic clove

2 small onions, thinly sliced

4 tbsp lemon juice

1 tbsp white wine vinegar

125 ml/4 fl oz olive oil

1 tbsp chopped fresh flat-leaf
　parsley

1 tsp chopped fresh mint

2 tsp chopped fresh dill

½ green pepper, thinly sliced

2 hard-boiled eggs, sliced,
　to garnish

method

1 Place the drained cannellini beans in a saucepan and cover with cold water. Bring to the boil, then cover the pan and boil gently for about 1 hour, or until the beans are tender but still firm. Add salt to taste about 15 minutes before the end of the cooking time. Drain the beans and transfer to a serving bowl.

2 Crush the garlic with a little salt using a pestle and mortar. Add the garlic to the hot beans with the onions, lemon juice, vinegar and olive oil. Stir gently to combine, then set aside until the beans are completely cool.

3 Gently stir in the chopped herbs and sliced pepper and chill in the refrigerator for 1 hour. Serve garnished with the egg slices.

cucumber & yogurt salad

ingredients

SERVES 6

1 large, firm cucumber,
    peeled, deseeded and
    diced

salt

2 garlic cloves

450 ml/16 fl oz Greek-style
    yogurt

white pepper

3 tbsp finely chopped fresh
    mint, plus extra sprigs
    to garnish

method

1 Sprinkle the diced cucumber with a little salt and drain in a colander for 30 minutes.

2 Crush the garlic with a little salt using a pestle and mortar. Stir in 2 tbsp of the yogurt, then add the mixture to the rest of the yogurt and stir well to combine. Season to taste with pepper and a little more salt, if liked. Stir in the chopped mint.

3 Drain the cucumber and stir into the yogurt. Chill in the refrigerator for 1 hour, then serve garnished with fresh mint sprigs.

cheese boreks

ingredients

MAKES 15

10 sheets of filo pastry,
    thawed if frozen
55 g/2 oz unsalted butter,
    melted
butter, for greasing

filling

175 g/6 oz feta cheese,
    crumbled
175 g/6 oz ricotta cheese
2 tbsp pine nuts, lightly
    toasted
4 tbsp finely chopped fresh
    flat-leaf parsley
1 small egg, beaten
pepper

method

1 Stack the filo pastry sheets and, using a sharp knife, cut the stack into 3 strips so that each strip is about 15 x 30 cm/6 x 12 inches. Cover the strips with a damp tea towel.

2 Place the feta and ricotta cheeses in a bowl and beat together to combine. Stir in the pine nuts, parsley, beaten egg and pepper to taste.

3 Lay a strip of filo pastry out on a work surface with a short side nearest to you, keeping the remaining sheets covered with the damp tea towel. Brush the filo strip with a little melted butter and place another strip of filo on top. Arrange about 1 tablespoon of the filling in a line along the short side, about 1 cm/$\frac{1}{2}$ inch in from the end and 2.5 cm/1 inch in from both long sides.

4 Make one tight roll to enclose the filling, then fold in both long sides for the length of the filo. Continue rolling up to the end. Use a little melted butter to seal the end. Place on a greased baking sheet and brush with melted butter. Repeat until all the filo and filling have been used up.

5 Bake the cheese boreks in a preheated oven, 180°C/350°F/Gas Mark 4, for about 20 minutes, or until crisp and golden brown. Serve hot.

hummus

ingredients

SERVES 6

225 g/8 oz chickpeas, soaked
   overnight and drained
3 medium garlic cloves
1½ tsp salt
150 ml/5 fl oz tahini
juice of 2 lemons
2 tbsp finely chopped fresh
   flat-leaf parsley, plus extra
   to garnish
pepper
pinch of cayenne pepper

method

1 Place the chickpeas in a large saucepan, cover with cold water and bring to the boil. Reduce the heat and boil gently for about 1½ hours, or until tender. Drain the chickpeas and set aside to cool.

2 Place the chickpeas in a food processor and process to a thick paste. Crush the garlic with the salt and add to the chickpeas with the tahini, lemon juice and parsley. Season to taste with pepper and a pinch of cayenne pepper, then process to combine thoroughly.

3 Chill in the refrigerator for 1–2 hours, then serve garnished with extra parsley.

fish balls

ingredients

SERVES 4–6

750 g/1 lb 8 oz white fish
 fillets, skinned and boned
3 tbsp chopped spring onions
1 tbsp chopped fresh flat-leaf
 parsley
1 tsp chopped fresh dill
85 g/3 oz fresh white
 breadcrumbs
1 egg, beaten
salt and pepper
plain flour, for coating
oil, for deep frying
lemon wedges, to serve

method

1 Roughly chop the fish fillets. Place them in a food processor with the spring onions, parsley and dill, and process to a paste.

2 Transfer the fish mixture to a large bowl and stir in most of the breadcrumbs and the beaten egg. Season with about 1 tsp of salt, and pepper to taste. Mix to a firm paste, adding a few more breadcrumbs if necessary.

3 Using damp hands, shape the mixture into small balls about the size of a walnut. Chill in the refrigerator for 30 minutes, until firm.

4 Sprinkle the flour on a plate and turn the fish balls in it to coat. Heat the oil for deep-frying in a large, heavy-based saucepan until a cube of day-old bread browns in 30 seconds. Deep-fry the fish balls, in batches, for 6–8 minutes, turning to brown evenly. Using a slotted spoon, remove from the pan and drain on kitchen paper. Serve hot with lemon wedges.

prawn balls

ingredients

SERVES 4

2 tbsp butter

3 tbsp flour

125 ml/4 fl oz milk

100 g/3½ oz peeled prawns,
    roughly chopped

1 tbsp lemon juice

salt and pepper

115 g/4 oz mozzarella
    cheese, grated

plain flour, for coating

1 egg

½ tsp olive oil

25 g/1 oz breadcrumbs

125 ml/4 fl oz oil, for frying

salad leaves, to serve

method

1 Melt the butter in a large saucepan over medium heat, add the flour and cook, stirring constantly, for 1 minute. Gradually add the milk, stirring constantly, and cook for 2 minutes until smooth. Add the chopped prawns, lemon juice and salt and pepper to taste and simmer for 3 minutes.

2 Remove the pan from the heat and immediately stir in the cheese. Allow to cool, then transfer the mixture to a bowl and chill in the refrigerator for 1 hour.

3 Sprinkle some flour on a large plate, place the mixture on it, and separate it into 12 balls the size of a walnut. Lightly beat the egg in a shallow dish and stir in the olive oil. Place the breadcrumbs in a separate shallow dish. Coat each prawn ball first in the beaten egg, then in the breadcrumbs.

4 Heat the oil in a heavy-based frying pan and fry the prawn balls, in batches, until golden. Using a slotted spoon, remove from the oil and drain on kitchen paper. Serve hot, with salad leaves.

cod roe dip

ingredients

SERVES 4

2 thick slices of white bread,
    crusts removed

milk, for soaking

85 g/3 oz smoked cod roe

1 garlic clove

1 tbsp grated onion

juice of 1 large lemon

4 tbsp olive oil

black olives, to garnish

crusty bread, to serve

method

1 Place the bread in a shallow bowl and pour in just enough milk to cover. Skin the cod roe and place it in a food processor. Squeeze the moisture out of the bread and add it to the cod's roe with the garlic and onion. Process until smooth.

2 Gradually add the lemon juice and olive oil to the mixture and process until a creamy paste is formed. Garnish with black olives and serve with bread.

cold cucumber soup

ingredients

SERVES 6

2 small, firm cucumbers

salt

750 ml/24 fl oz plain yogurt

2–3 garlic cloves, crushed

2 tbsp finely chopped fresh
    mint

3 tbsp olive oil

250 ml/8 fl oz very cold water

freshly ground white pepper

ice cubes, to serve

fresh mint sprigs, to garnish

method

1 Grate the cucumbers into a colander, gently mix in 1 teaspoon of salt and drain for 20 minutes.

2 Transfer the cucumber to a large serving bowl and add the yogurt, garlic, mint and olive oil. Cover and chill in the refrigerator for at least 2 hours.

3 When you are ready to serve, pour in just enough very cold water to give a creamy consistency. Taste and season with salt, if necessary, and pepper. Serve immediately with ice cubes and garnished with fresh sprigs of mint.

spinach soup

ingredients

SERVES 4

450 g/1 lb fresh spinach
    leaves
1.2 litres/40 fl oz chicken
    stock
salt and pepper
1 carrot, peeled and julienned
1 celery stalk, chopped
2 tbsp butter
2 tbsp flour
2 large egg yolks
juice of 1 lemon

method

1 Wash the spinach thoroughly, then drain and finely chop the leaves.

2 Bring the chicken stock to the boil in a large saucepan and season to taste with salt and pepper. Add the carrot and celery, reduce the heat and simmer for about 15 minutes, or until the vegetables are nearly cooked. Add the chopped spinach and continue to simmer for a further 5 minutes.

3 Meanwhile, melt the butter in a small saucepan, blend in the flour and cook over low heat, stirring constantly, for 2–3 minutes. Add a ladleful of the soup, stirring constantly, then add the mixture to the soup, a little at a time and continue to stir constantly. Simmer over low heat for 10 minutes.

4 Place the egg yolks and lemon juice in a bowl and beat together to combine. Add a ladleful of the soup and beat thoroughly. Gradually return the mixture to the soup, stirring constantly. Bring the soup to just below boiling point, then remove from the heat immediately and serve at once, garnished with chopped parsley.

wedding soup

ingredients

SERVES 4

350 g/12 oz lean, boneless
    lamb, cut into 2.5-cm/
    1-inch cubes
3 tbsp plain flour
2 tbsp butter
2 tbsp olive oil
350 g/12 oz lamb marrow
    bones
1.3 litres/48 fl oz water
1 onion, cut into quarters
1 carrot, cut into quarters
salt and pepper
pinch of cayenne pepper
2 small egg yolks
2 tbsp lemon juice
1½ tbsp melted butter mixed
    with 1½ tsp paprika,
        to garnish

method

1 Toss the cubed lamb in the flour until coated. Heat the butter and olive oil in a large, heavy-based saucepan and cook the lamb until lightly browned all over. Add the marrow bones and water to the pan and bring to the boil.

2 Skim off any scum that rises to the surface and add the onion and carrot. Season to taste with salt, pepper and a pinch of cayenne pepper, if liked. Cover the pan and simmer gently for about 1½ hours, or until the meat is very tender. Remove the meat with a slotted spoon, remove and discard the bones, then strain the stock and discard the vegetables. Return the stock to a clean pan and let it simmer gently.

3 Just before serving, beat the egg yolks, then add the lemon juice and beat again. Beat in a ladleful of the hot stock, then gradually add the mixture to the stock, beating constantly. Return the meat to the stock and heat, stirring constantly, until the egg is cooked. Do not allow the soup to boil. Taste and adjust the seasoning if necessary.

4 Serve the soup immediately, garnished with the melted paprika-butter.

chicken & yogurt soup with rice

ingredients

SERVES 6

750 ml//25 fl oz chicken stock

salt and pepper

55 g/2 oz long-grain white rice

750 ml/25 fl oz yogurt

1 tbsp cornflour dissolved
    in 125 ml/4 fl oz cold
    water

2 egg yolks, lightly beaten

2 tbsp butter

2 tbsp dried mint

crusty bread, to serve

method

1 Put the chicken stock in a large, heavy-based saucepan, season to taste with salt and pepper and bring to the boil. Add the rice, reduce the heat and simmer for about 15 minutes, or until the rice is almost tender.

2 Meanwhile, beat the yogurt with the cornflour mixture, then add the egg yolks and beat again. Place in a large, heavy-based saucepan over medium heat and bring slowly to the boil. When the mixture thickens, add it slowly to the stock and rice, stirring constantly, and simmer until the rice is cooked.

3 Just before serving, melt the butter in a small saucepan and stir in the dried mint. Drizzle over the soup and serve with crusty bread.

fish soup

ingredients

SERVES 6

3 tbsp olive oil

2 large onions, finely chopped

1.75 litres/65 fl oz fish stock

3 tbsp white wine vinegar

1 garlic clove

2 tbsp chopped fresh flat-leaf
    parsley

salt and pepper

450 g/1 lb white fish fillets,
    skinned, boned and cut
    into 2.5-cm/1-inch chunks

3 egg yolks

juice of 1 lemon

ground cinnamon, for dusting

method

1 Heat the olive oil in a large saucepan and cook the onions until softened but not browned. Add the fish stock, vinegar, garlic, parsley and salt and pepper to taste, bring to the boil, then simmer for 30 minutes. Strain the stock through a fine sieve and return to a clean pan.

2 Bring the stock back to the boil, then add the chunks of fish and simmer over low heat for about 15 minutes, or until the flesh flakes easily. Remove the fish carefully using a slotted spoon, cover and keep warm.

3 Beat the egg yolks, then add the lemon juice and beat again. Beat in a ladleful of the hot stock and return the mixture to the soup, beating constantly. Heat the soup to just below boiling point, then return the fish to the soup. Serve immediately, garnished with a dusting of ground cinnamon.

meat
& poultry

Turkish meat and poultry dishes are wonderfully creative and, in addition to the meat, include the full range of typical ingredients. Aubergines, peppers and tomatoes are ideal for stuffing with a minced-meat filling, and recipes for all three are included here. An unusual variation on this theme is Spicy Lamb-and-Rice-Stuffed Apricots, a combination that sounds most unlikely but is succulent and delicious.

Yogurt is used in all Turkish cooking, from soups to cakes. It can be flavoured with garlic and served to accompany kebabs or other meat dishes, and takes a starring role in Lamb Dumplings in Yogurt Sauce – plump little parcels that are just delectable!

Kebabs are one of those dishes that most people recognize as being Turkish. Doner kebabs are perhaps the most well-known, usually seen rotating tantalizingly on a spit in a restaurant window and, unfortunately, impossible to make at home without special equipment. However, kebab-lovers will find in this chapter recipes for two other classics, Shish Kebab and Kofta.

If you've never tried okra before, Chicken Casserole with Okra is the perfect introduction. Other chicken recipes include a simple but extremely tasty Chicken Pilaf and, to ring the changes, Bulgar Pilaf with Chicken – it's very good!

shish kebab

ingredients

SERVES 4

900 g/2 lb leg of lamb, cut
into 2-cm/¾-inch cubes
16 pearl onions, left whole
16 cherry tomatoes, left whole
1 red pepper, halved,
deseeded and each half
cut into 8 pieces
freshly cooked white rice and
salad leaves, to serve

marinade

150 ml/5 fl oz olive oil
2 onions
1 tsp ground cinnamon
salt and pepper

method

1 To make the marinade, place the olive oil in a shallow, non-metallic dish, grate in the onions, add the cinnamon and season to taste with salt and pepper. Add the cubes of lamb, stir to coat thoroughly and set aside to marinate for at least 3 hours, or overnight.

2 Just before cooking the kebabs, blanch the onions in boiling salted water for 5 minutes, then drain well.

3 Drain the lamb cubes and thread them onto 8 flat metal skewers, alternating the lamb with the tomatoes, onions and pepper pieces.

4 Cook the skewers under a preheated grill for 7–10 minutes, turning frequently and brushing with the marinade occasionally, until the meat is a rich golden brown on the outside but still pink and moist inside.

5 Serve immediately on a bed of freshly cooked rice, with salad to accompany.

lamb kebabs with yogurt

ingredients

SERVES 4

2 tbsp olive oil

3 tbsp plus 1 tsp butter

450 g/1 lb lean lamb, cut into
2.5-cm/1-inch cubes

salt and pepper

4 tomatoes, peeled and
chopped

300 ml/10 fl oz yogurt

4 thick slices of bread, crusts
removed

2 tsp paprika

method

1 Heat the olive oil and 2 tablespoons of the butter in a heavy-based frying pan over medium–low heat and cook the lamb cubes, stirring frequently, until just tender. Season to taste with salt and pepper.

2 Meanwhile, melt the teaspoon of butter in a saucepan over medium–low heat, stir in the tomatoes and cook until very soft. Season to taste with salt and pepper. Beat the yogurt until smooth and season to taste. Toast the bread slices lightly on both sides, then cut into 2.5-cm/1-inch squares and arrange on a serving plate. Melt the remaining tablespoon of butter and stir in the paprika.

3 To serve, spread the tomatoes over the bread squares, pour over the yogurt, top with the lamb cubes and drizzle with the paprika butter. Serve immediately.

spiced lamb & chickpeas

ingredients

SERVES 6

175 g/6 oz chickpeas

4 tbsp olive oil

900 g/2 lb boned shoulder
of lamb, cut into
2.5-cm/1-inch cubes

1 large onion, thinly sliced

350 g/12 oz aubergine, cut
into 1.5-cm/½-inch cubes

1 tsp ground allspice

450 g/1 lb tomatoes, peeled
and thickly sliced

2 garlic cloves, crushed

2 tbsp finely chopped fresh
mint

150 ml/5 fl oz yogurt

spicy pilaf, to serve (see page
148)

method

1 Place the chickpeas in a large saucepan,
pour in 1 litre/32 fl oz of boiling water, then
cover and set aside to soak for 3 hours. Drain,
cover with fresh cold water and bring to the
boil. Cover the pan and boil for about 1 hour,
or until the chickpeas are tender but still firm.
Remove from the heat and set aside.

2 Heat the oil in a large, heavy-based
saucepan, add the lamb cubes and cook, in
batches, over high heat until browned all over.
Remove the lamb from the pan using a slotted
spoon and set aside.

3 Add the onion and aubergine to the pan
and cook, stirring, for about 5 minutes or
until lightly coloured. Add the allspice and
cook for a further 1 minute, then add
the tomatoes, garlic and mint. Drain the
chickpeas, reserving the cooking liquid, and
add them to the pan with the lamb. Pour
in about 500 ml/16 fl oz of the reserved
chickpea cooking liquid and stir thoroughly.

4 Bring to a simmer over medium–low heat,
then reduce the heat to low, cover and
simmer very gently for 30 minutes. Remove
the lid and cook for a further 45 minutes, or
until the meat is very tender and the sauce
has thickened. Stir in the yogurt and serve
immediately with spicy pilaf.

lamb dumplings in yogurt sauce

ingredients

SERVES 4

250 ml/8 fl oz chicken stock
500 ml/16 fl oz Greek-style
    yogurt
2 garlic cloves, crushed
2 tsp dried mint
fresh mint leaves, to garnish

dough

300 g/10 oz plain flour
½ tsp salt
1 egg, beaten with cold water
    to make 125 ml/4 fl oz

filling

175 g/6 oz minced lamb
1 small onion, grated
2 tbsp finely chopped fresh
    flat-leaf parsley
salt and pepper

method

1 To make the dough, sift the flour and salt into a bowl. Stir the egg mixture into the flour and mix to a firm dough. Knead until smooth, then cover with a damp tea towel and rest for 30 minutes.

2 Meanwhile, to make the filling, place the lamb, grated onion and parsley in a bowl, season with salt and pepper and stir well.

3 Roll out the dough very thinly on a lightly floured work surface. Cut into 5-cm/2-inch squares and cover with a damp tea towel.

4 Place 1 teaspoon of filling in the centre of 1 square, moisten the edges with water and fold over to make a triangle. Press to seal the edges, then fold in the bottom angles of the triangle and press together to seal. Place on a tea towel while you make the remainder.

5 Bring a large pan of salted water to the boil, add the dumplings, return to the boil and boil for 5 minutes. Remove with a slotted spoon.

6 Bring the chicken stock to the boil in a large saucepan, add the dumplings, and simmer for 5 minutes. Stir the garlic and dried mint into the yogurt, add to the pan and heat through gently. Do not allow the sauce to boil. Serve immediately, garnished with fresh mint leaves.

spicy lamb-and rice-stuffed apricots

ingredients

SERVES 6

55 g/2 oz long-grain white rice

18 large pitted dried apricots, rinsed

2 tbsp olive oil

175 g/6 oz minced lamb

½ tsp ground allspice

salt and pepper

1 tbsp butter

2 tbsp sugar

6 tbsp water

method

1 Place the rice in a bowl, cover in boiling water and set aside for 20 minutes. Rinse under cold running water and drain well.

2 Place the apricots in a bowl, cover in warm water and soak for 10 minutes. Transfer the apricots and the soaking liquid to a pan, bring to the boil, then reduce the heat and simmer for 15 minutes. Drain thoroughly.

3 Heat the olive oil in a frying pan over medium heat, then add the meat and cook, stirring, for 2–3 minutes. Remove from the heat and stir in the rice. Cool, then add the allspice, season to taste and mix well. Slit open the apricots and divide the filling between them.

4 Melt the butter in a wide, shallow saucepan. Remove from the heat and arrange the stuffed apricots on the bottom. Bring the sugar and water to the boil in a pan, stirring. Remove from the heat when the sugar has dissolved and pour the syrup over the apricots.

5 Bring the syrup to the boil, reduce the heat to medium and cook for 5 minutes. Cover the pan, reduce the heat to medium–low and cook for a further 30 minutes, lifting the lid occasionally to release the steam. Remove the pan from the heat and let stand, covered, for 10 minutes. Serve warm or cold.

lamb with smoked aubergine

ingredients

SERVES 4

2 tbsp olive oil

2 large onions, peeled and
  roughly chopped

450 g/1 lb lean lamb, cut into
  2.5-cm/1-inch cubes

salt and pepper

400 g/14 oz canned chopped
  tomatoes

½ tsp ground cumin

½ tsp paprika

425 ml/15 fl oz lamb stock

small bunch of fresh flat-leaf
  parsley, finely chopped

sauce

3 medium aubergines, rinsed
  and dried

juice of 2 large lemons

1 tbsp butter

1 tbsp plain flour

300 ml/10 fl oz milk

55 g/2 oz Kashkaval cheese,
  grated

method

1 To prepare the sauce, place the aubergines under a grill preheated to the highest setting. Grill, turning frequently, until the skins are black and starting to blister and the flesh has softened. Cool slightly, then rub the skins off under cold running water. Place in a large bowl with the lemon juice and enough cold water to cover. Soak for 30 minutes, then drain the aubergines and squeeze out as much water as possible. Mash the flesh with a fork and set aside.

2 Meanwhile, heat the oil in a large saucepan. Add the onions and cook, stirring occasionally, for 5 minutes, or until just starting to brown. Add the lamb cubes and season to taste. Cook for 5 minutes, stirring frequently, until the lamb is browned all over. Stir in the tomatoes, cumin, paprika and stock, bring to the boil, then reduce the heat and simmer for 1 hour, or until the meat is tender and the sauce has thickened. Stir in the parsley and keep warm.

3 To finish the sauce, melt the butter in a saucepan and stir in the flour. Cook, stirring, for 1 minute, then gradually add the milk and cook over medium heat, stirring, until the sauce is smooth and creamy. Stir in the grated cheese, then add the mashed aubergine and stir well. Serve immediately, with the lamb.

lamb pilaf

ingredients

SERVES 6

3 tbsp olive oil

1 large onion, finely chopped

450 g/1 lb lean lamb, cut into
   1.5-cm/½-inch pieces

½ tsp ground cinnamon

salt and pepper

2 tbsp tomato paste

2 tbsp finely chopped fresh
   flat-leaf parsley

2 tbsp pine nuts

2 tbsp raisins

450 g/1 lb long-grain rice,
   rinsed and drained

method

1 Heat the olive oil in a large, heavy-based saucepan, add the onion and cook for 5 minutes, or until softened and lightly coloured. Add the lamb pieces and cook for a further 5 minutes, or until they are browned all over. Add the cinnamon and season to taste with salt and pepper. Cover and cook over low heat, stirring occasionally, for 10 minutes.

2 Stir in the tomato paste, then add enough cold water to cover the mixture. Stir in the chopped parsley, pine nuts and raisins, bring to the boil, then reduce the heat and simmer for about 1½ hours, or until the meat is tender and the sauce has thickened.

3 Add about 425 ml/15 fl oz of water to the pan, then gently stir in the rice. Bring to the boil, then reduce the heat, cover and simmer without stirring for about 20 minutes, or until the rice is cooked, adding a little boiling water if necessary. Remove the pilaf from the heat and let it stand for 5 minutes before serving.

kofta

ingredients

SERVES 4

900 g/2 lb very finely minced
    beef
2 medium onions, grated
½ tsp ground cumin
½ tsp ground coriander
1 egg
salt and pepper
pitta bread and salad leaves,
    to serve

sauce

250 ml/8 fl oz Greek-style
    yogurt
2 tbsp chopped fresh mint

method

1 Place the minced beef in a bowl and stir in the onion, cumin, coriander and egg and season to taste with salt and pepper. Pound the mixture with a wooden spoon or knead with your hands until very smooth.

2 Divide the meat mixture into 4 and form it into sausage shapes around 4 flat metal skewers.

3 Cook the kofta under a preheated grill for 3–5 minutes, turning occasionally, until brown all over and cooked through. Alternatively cook the kofta on a barbecue, making sure the wire rack is well oiled to prevent the meat from sticking.

4 Meanwhile, stir the chopped fresh mint into the yogurt and set aside.

5 Serve the skewers immediately, with pitta bread, salad leaves and a bowl of yogurt sauce to accompany.

stuffed aubergines

ingredients

SERVES 4

2 large aubergines

6 tbsp olive oil

2 small onions, finely
    chopped

350 g/12 oz minced beef

salt and pepper

2 tomatoes, peeled, deseeded
    and chopped

1 tsp tomato paste

115 g/4 oz Kashkaval cheese,
    grated

freshly cooked rice, to serve

method

1 Cut the aubergines in half lengthways and scoop out the centres. Sprinkle the cavities with a little salt and drain in a colander for 30 minutes.

2 Meanwhile, heat 2 tablespoons of the oil in a frying pan, add the onions and cook for about 5 minutes, stirring occasionally, until softened but not browned. Add the minced beef and cook, stirring, until it changes colour. Season to taste with salt and pepper.

3 Add the tomatoes and tomato paste to the frying pan with 4 tablespoons of water, stir and simmer until the tomatoes are cooked and a thick sauce has formed. Stir in the grated cheese and remove from the heat.

4 Rinse the aubergines and pat dry, then arrange them in an ovenproof dish and divide the filling between them. Mix 150 ml/5 fl oz of water with the remaining olive oil and pour around the aubergines. Bake in a preheated oven, 200°C/400°F/Gas Mark 6, for 15 minutes, then reduce the temperature to 170°C/325°F/Gas Mark 3 and cook for a further 30–45 minutes, or until the aubergines are tender. Serve with freshly cooked rice.

stuffed peppers

ingredients

SERVES 4

4 tbsp olive oil

225 g/8 oz long-grain rice

500 ml/16 fl oz boiling water

salt and pepper

2 medium onions, peeled
   and chopped

2 garlic cloves, crushed

350 g/12 oz minced beef

2 tbsp currants

2 tbsp pine nuts

½ tsp ground cinnamon

½ tsp dried marjoram

400 g/14 oz canned tomatoes

2 tbsp tomato paste

4 medium red peppers

method

1 Heat 2 tablespoons of the oil in a saucepan over medium heat. Add the rice and stir well to coat, then pour in the boiling water and add a little salt. Stir once, then cover the pan and simmer for 15 minutes, or until the water has been absorbed. Remove from the heat.

2 Meanwhile, heat the remaining oil in a large, heavy-based saucepan over medium heat. Add the onions and garlic and cook, stirring, for 5 minutes. Add the minced beef and cook until the colour changes. Stir in the currants, pine nuts, cinnamon and marjoram and season to taste with salt and pepper. Add two of the tomatoes with a little of the juice from the can, and the tomato paste, and stir to combine. Reduce the heat and simmer until the sauce has thickened.

3 To prepare the peppers, cut off and retain the stalk ends. Pull out the core and seeds, then rinse and drain the peppers and place them in an ovenproof casserole.

4 Add the cooked rice to the meat mixture, then divide the filling between the peppers and replace the stalks. Spoon any leftover filling around the peppers and add the remaining tomatoes and can juices. Cover and cook in a preheated oven, 190°C/375°F/ Gas Mark 5, for about 45 minutes, or until the peppers are tender. Serve immediately.

stuffed tomatoes

ingredients

SERVES 6

12 large, ripe, firm tomatoes

3 tbsp olive oil

salt

sprigs of fresh dill, to garnish

filling

2 tbsp olive oil

2 medium onions, thinly
    sliced

55 g/2 oz long-grain rice,
    rinsed and drained

250 ml/8 fl oz water

350 g/12 oz minced beef
    or lamb

4 tbsp chopped fresh dill

salt and pepper

method

1 Cut off the stalk ends of the tomatoes and set aside. Scoop out and discard the seeds, then scoop out the tomato flesh and reserve in a bowl.

2 To make the filling, heat the oil in a saucepan, add the onions and cook for 5–7 minutes over medium–high heat, until softened and turning golden. Add the drained rice and stir to coat it in oil, then add the water. Cover the pan, reduce the heat to medium and simmer for 10 minutes, or until the water has been absorbed.

3 Remove the pan from the heat and stir in the minced meat and dill. Season to taste with salt and pepper and mix thoroughly. Chop the reserved tomato flesh and add it to the meat mixture.

4 Divide the filling between the tomatoes, replace the stalk ends and place the tomatoes in a saucepan large enough to hold them firmly in a single layer. Mix the olive oil and a little salt with 250 ml/8 fl oz of water and pour the mixture around the tomatoes. Cover the pan and cook over medium heat for 30 minutes, or until the tomatoes are tender. Transfer to a serving dish and garnish with fresh dill sprigs.

beef & feta croquettes

ingredients

SERVES 4

675 g/1 lb 8 oz beef, very
   finely minced

1 medium onion, grated

55 g/2 oz feta cheese,
   crumbled

2 tbsp long-grain white rice

1 tbsp finely chopped fresh
   flat-leaf parsley

1 tsp finely chopped fresh dill

salt and pepper

3 eggs

1 tsp olive oil

oil, for frying

plain flour, for coating

tomato salad, to serve (see
   page 146), optional

method

1 Place the minced beef, onion and cheese in a food processor and process to thoroughly combine. Transfer to a mixing bowl, add the rice, parsley and dill, and season to taste with salt and pepper. Lightly beat 2 of the eggs with the olive oil and knead into the meat mixture to make a smooth paste.

2 Using damp hands, take a generous tablespoon of the mixture and form it into an elongated oval shape. When all the croquettes have been formed, place them in a saucepan large enough to hold them in a single layer, pour in about 300 ml/10 fl oz of water, bring to a simmer over medium heat, cover and simmer for about 20 minutes, until the water has been absorbed and the meat and rice are cooked. Drain the croquettes and cool.

3 Lightly beat the egg in a shallow dish and sprinkle a thick layer of flour on a plate. Dip each croquette into the beaten egg and turn to coat completely, then turn it in the flour to coat thoroughly.

4 Heat enough oil over medium–high heat to coat the bottom of a large frying pan. Drop the croquettes into the hot oil, in batches, and cook, turning frequently with tongs, until they are crisp and golden brown all over. Remove with a slotted spoon and drain on kitchen paper. Serve immediately with a tomato salad, if using.

meatballs in tomato sauce

ingredients

SERVES 4

2 thick slices day-old white
   bread
675 g/1 lb 8 oz beef, very
   finely minced
1 garlic clove, crushed
1 small onion
1 egg
1 tsp ground cumin
2 tbsp chopped fresh flat-leaf
   parsley
salt and pepper
plain flour, for coating
4 tbsp olive oil
freshly cooked rice, to serve

tomato sauce

350 g/12 oz tomatoes, peeled
   and chopped
2 tbsp tomato paste
1 tsp sugar
salt and pepper
250 ml/8 fl oz water

method

1 Place the bread in a shallow bowl and pour over enough water to cover. Soak for 10 minutes, then squeeze out the excess moisture. Place the minced beef and garlic in a mixing bowl, grate in the onion and stir to combine. Crumble in the bread, then add the egg, cumin and parsley, and season to taste with salt and pepper. Knead thoroughly to make a smooth paste.

2 Using damp hands, form the mixture into plump oval shapes. Sprinkle flour onto a plate and coat the meatballs thoroughly.

3 Heat the olive oil in a large, heavy-based pan, add the meatballs in batches and cook, turning occasionally, until lightly browned all over. Remove and drain on kitchen paper.

4 When all the meatballs have been cooked, add the tomatoes and tomato paste to the pan and cook, stirring, over medium heat for about 5 minutes, or until the tomatoes have softened. Add the sugar and season to taste, then stir in the water and bring to the boil.

5 Return the meatballs to the pan and coat gently in the sauce. Cover and simmer for 1 hour, or until the meatballs are cooked and the sauce has thickened. If necessary, remove the lid and increase the heat slightly to reduce the sauce. Serve immediately, with freshly cooked rice.

meatballs with aubergine sauce

ingredients

SERVES 6

4 large aubergines

900 g/2 lb beef, very finely
    minced

2 eggs, beaten

3 tbsp white breadcrumbs

½ tsp ground cumin

½ tsp ground allspice

salt and pepper

plain flour, for coating

oil, for frying

1 onion, sliced

2 tbsp tomato paste

chunks of country bread, to
    serve (see page 162)

method

1 Rinse the aubergines, pat them dry and place them under a grill preheated to the highest setting. Grill the aubergines, turning frequently, until the skins are black and starting to blister and the flesh has softened. Cool slightly, then rub the skins off under cold running water. Gently squeeze out as much of the juice as possible, then place the flesh in a bowl and mash with a fork.

2 Knead the minced beef to form a very smooth paste. Stir in the eggs, breadcrumbs, cumin, allspice and season to taste with salt and pepper. Knead again then form the mixture into small balls and roll them in flour to coat. Heat 2–3 tablespoons of oil in a frying pan and fry the meatballs, in batches, on all sides until cooked through and browned all over. Remove from the pan with a slotted spoon and drain on kitchen paper.

3 Add the onion to the pan and cook over medium heat for about 5 minutes, or until softened and pale golden. Stir in the mashed aubergine flesh and the tomato paste, season to taste with salt and pepper and simmer for 10 minutes. Gently stir in the meatballs and simmer for a further 10 minutes. Serve immediately, accompanied with chunks of country bread.

borek pie

ingredients

MAKES 12 SQUARES

2 eggs

3 tbsp olive oil

150 ml/5 fl oz milk

125 ml/4 fl oz water

450 g/1 lb filo pastry

butter, for greasing

filling

½ tbsp olive oil

1 medium onion, finely
    chopped

225 g/8 oz minced beef

salt and pepper

2 tomatoes, peeled and
    chopped

1 small sweet pepper,
    chopped

method

1 To make the filling, heat the olive oil in a large saucepan, add the onion and cook over medium heat for 5 minutes, until softened. Add the beef and cook for 5 minutes, or until it has changed colour. Season to taste, then add the tomatoes and pepper and cook until the liquid has evaporated. Set aside.

2 Place the eggs, olive oil, milk and water in a bowl and whisk together. Unwrap the filo pastry and cover with a damp tea towel. Grease a shallow 32 x 22-cm/13 x 9-inch baking dish with butter. Place 2 filo sheets in the bottom of the dish, leaving the edges of the pastry overlapping the sides of the dish. Brush the filo sheets with a little of the egg mixture. Take another 2 filo sheets, fold them in half and place in the dish. Brush with a little of the egg mixture, then continue adding layers of 2 folded filo sheets, brushing each layer with the egg mixture, until half the filo sheets have been used.

3 Spread the beef filling over the pastry, then continue adding layers of 2 folded filo sheets, brushing each layer with the egg mixture, until all the filo sheets have been used. Fold in the overhanging edges of pastry and brush the top with the remaining egg mixture. Chill for 2 hours, then bake in a preheated oven, 180°C/350°F/Gas Mark 4, for 20 minutes, until crisp and golden. Cool, then serve, cut into squares.

chicken skewers

ingredients

SERVES 4

675 g/1 lb 8 oz chicken
   breast, cut into 4-cm/
   1½-inch cubes
lemon wedges (optional) and
   warm pitta bread, to serve

marinade

1 tsp tomato paste
2 garlic cloves, crushed
1 small onion, grated
2 tbsp olive oil
2 tbsp lemon juice
salt and freshly ground
   white pepper

yogurt sauce

300 ml/10 fl oz plain yogurt
2 garlic cloves, crushed
salt and pepper
1 small cucumber, peeled,
   deseeded and cut into
   very small dice

method

1 Whisk the marinade ingredients together to make a thick paste. Place the marinade in a shallow, non-metallic bowl and mix in the chicken cubes, stirring well to coat. Cover and marinate in the refrigerator for at least 2 hours, but preferably overnight.

2 To make the yogurt sauce, place the yogurt in a bowl, stir in the crushed garlic, season to taste with salt and pepper, then stir in the diced cucumber. Chill in the refrigerator.

3 Thread the chicken cubes onto 4 wooden skewers that have been soaked in water for 30 minutes. Cook the skewers under a grill preheated to its highest setting for 10–15 minutes, turning frequently, until the meat is cooked through. Serve immediately, with warm pitta bread, the yogurt sauce and lemon wedges, if using.

chicken casserole with okra

ingredients

SERVES 4

450 g/1 lb okra

125 ml/4 fl oz white vinegar

salt and pepper

2 tbsp olive oil

2 tbsp butter

4 chicken portions, each
    weighing about 175 g/6 oz

1 onion, finely chopped

1 garlic clove, crushed

400 g/14 oz canned chopped
    tomatoes

1 tbsp tomato paste

125 ml/4 fl oz water

1 tsp sugar

1 bay leaf

method

1 Trim the stalks from the okra, leaving the conical end of the stalks in place, then carefully trim off the fibrous layer around the conical end, taking care not to pierce the pods. Place the vinegar in a shallow bowl, add 1 tsp of salt, then coat the okra in the mixture using your hands. Let stand for 30 minutes, then rinse and drain the okra.

2 Heat the olive oil and butter in a large saucepan over medium–high heat, add the chicken portions, and cook for about 3 minutes, or until browned all over. Remove and set aside.

3 Reduce the heat, add the onions and cook for 5 minutes, until softened. Add the garlic and cook for 30 seconds, then add the tomatoes with their can juices, tomato paste, water, sugar and bay leaf. Season to taste, then add the chicken, turning to coat it in the sauce. Cover and simmer for 20 minutes.

4 Arrange the okra on top of the chicken but do not coat it in the sauce. Cover and cook for a further 20 minutes, or until the okra and the chicken are tender.

5 Remove the okra from the pan using a slotted spoon. Transfer the chicken and sauce to a warm serving dish and serve with the okra.

circassian chicken

ingredients

SERVES 6

1 chicken, weighing about
　1.4 kg/3 lb

1 large onion, cut into
　quarters

1 carrot, cut into quarters

2 sprigs of fresh flat-leaf
　parsley

salt and freshly ground white
　pepper

3 slices day-old white bread,
　crusts removed

175 g/6 oz walnuts, finely
　chopped

½ tsp paprika

1 clove of garlic, crushed

½ tsp paprika steeped in
　1 tbsp walnut oil, to serve

method

1 Place the chicken, onion, carrot, parsley and just enough cold water to cover in a saucepan over medium heat. Bring slowly to simmering point, skimming the surface if necessary. Season to taste, then cover and simmer over very low heat for about 1½ hours, or until the chicken is tender and cooked through.

2 Allow to cool, then transfer the chicken to a plate, remove the meat and set aside. Return the skin and carcass to the pan, bring to the boil and boil until the stock is reduced by half. Strain and reserve the stock, discarding the skin and carcass. Cut the chicken meat into 5-cm/2-inch strips and place in a bowl. Pour over 2 tablespoons of the stock, then cover and chill in the refrigerator.

3 Meanwhile, soak the bread in enough stock to cover it, then squeeze out the excess moisture and crumble the bread into a food processor. Add the walnuts, paprika and garlic and process briefly to combine. Gradually pour in about 250 ml/8 fl oz of warm stock to make a smooth, thick sauce. Taste and adjust the seasoning if necessary.

4 Mix one-third of the sauce into the chicken, then spread the remaining sauce over the chicken. Cover with clingfilm and chill in the refrigerator. Serve cold, drizzled with the paprika-walnut oil.

chicken pilaf

ingredients

SERVES 4

1 roasting chicken, weighing
    about 1.8 kg/4 lb
2 tbsp olive oil
salt and black pepper
½ tsp dried parsley
½ tsp dried dill
450 g/1 lb long-grain rice,
    rinsed and drained

method

1 Rinse the chicken and pat dry thoroughly with kitchen paper.

2 Heat the olive oil in a large, heavy-based saucepan and fry the chicken, turning frequently, until browned all over. Add just enough water to cover, season to taste with salt and pepper and add the dried herbs. Bring to the boil, reduce the heat and simmer for about 1 hour, or until very tender. Remove from the heat, cool a little, then remove the chicken from the stock and set aside.

3 When it is cool enough to handle, cut the chicken meat into pieces. Set aside the larger pieces, moisten them with a little stock and cover. Measure the stock and either add water or boil the stock vigorously to reduce it, to make the same volume of stock as of rice.

4 Return the smaller chicken pieces to the stock, add the rice, stir and bring to the boil. Reduce the heat, cover and simmer gently for 20 minutes, without stirring, until the rice is tender. Transfer to a serving dish, arrange the reserved chicken pieces on top and serve immediately.

bulgar pilaf with chicken

ingredients

SERVES 4

85 g/3 oz butter

4 tbsp olive oil

2 onions, finely chopped

675 g/1 lb 8 oz chicken
    breast, cut into
    2.5-cm/1-inch chunks

salt and pepper

3 tomatoes, peeled and
    chopped

5 tbsp tomato paste

450 g/1 lb bulgar wheat

method

1 Melt 25 g/1 oz of the butter with 2 tablespoons of the olive oil in a large, heavy-based saucepan over medium heat. Add the onions and cook, stirring occasionally, for 5 minutes or until just beginning to colour. Add the chicken to the pan and cook, stirring frequently, until golden.

2 Season to taste with salt and pepper. Add the chopped tomatoes and tomato paste, and pour in just enough water to cover. Simmer gently for 30–45 minutes, or until the chicken is very tender, adding more water if necessary.

3 Meanwhile, melt the remaining butter with the remaining oil in another large saucepan. Add the bulgar and cook, stirring constantly, for 10 minutes. Remove from the heat, add salt to taste, then add the meat. Make the meat sauce up to 600 ml/20 fl oz with boiling water and stir into the bulgar wheat.

4 Cover the pan, return to the heat and simmer gently for 10 minutes, or until the liquid has been absorbed. Remove the pan from the heat, remove the lid, stretch a clean tea towel over the pan and replace the lid. Reduce the heat to its lowest setting and return the pan, using a heat diffuser if you have one. Steam the pilaf for 30 minutes, or until the bulgar wheat is soft. Serve at once.

fish
& seafood

It is perhaps in its fish and seafood dishes that Turkey most reflects the culinary style of its Mediterranean neighbours. Fish is cooked quickly, simply and is extremely fresh – Turkish cooks often adapt their recipes to make best use of the catch of the day, and you can do the same where appropriate. The easiest ways to cook fish are steaming or baking it in a paper package, or making it into a delectable stew, and there are recipes for all three methods here.

Fish lends itself to a variety of appetizing sauces. Make use of a glut of well-flavoured tomatoes to make Baked Fish with Tomato Sauce or Fish Steaks with Tomato Sauce, simple recipes that look and taste great, and are light and nutritious dishes for when time is short. Red Snapper Fillets with Lemon Cream Sauce and Sea Bass with Almond Sauce are rather more sophisticated and perfect for serving to guests.

To accompany your favourite unadorned fish, learn to make Hazelnut Sauce – the recipe is given on page 156 – or Tahini & Walnut Sauce, on page 158. In this chapter these gorgeous sauces accompany Stuffed Mussels and Fried Mussels respectively, but they go equally well with simple baked or steamed fish and turn an ordinary dish into a very special one.

swordfish skewers

ingredients

SERVES 4

900 g/2 lb swordfish,
   skinned and cut into
   3-cm/1¼-inch cubes
freshly cooked rice, to serve

marinade

4 tbsp lemon juice

2 tbsp olive oil

1 small onion

1 tsp paprika

salt and pepper

2 tsp crushed dried
   bay leaves

lemon sauce

2 tbsp olive oil

2 tbsp lemon juice

1 tbsp finely chopped fresh
   flat-leaf parsley

salt and pepper

method

1 To make the marinade, place the lemon juice and olive oil in a shallow, non-metallic dish. Grate in the onion, then stir in the paprika, salt and pepper to taste, and crushed bay leaves. Add the swordfish cubes, coat thoroughly in the marinade, then cover and marinate in the refrigerator for 2 hours.

2 Thread the swordfish cubes onto 4 wooden skewers that have been soaked in water for 30 minutes, and cook under a preheated grill for about 10 minutes until cooked through, turning frequently and basting with the marinade. Alternatively, cook on a barbecue over hot coals.

3 To make the sauce, whisk together the olive oil, lemon juice and parsley and season to taste with salt and pepper.

4 Serve the swordfish skewers on a bed of rice, with the lemon sauce to accompany.

fish steaks steamed in paper

ingredients

SERVES 4

olive oil, for brushing

4 tbsp chopped spring onions

4 tbsp finely chopped fresh
    flat-leaf parsley

4 thick white fish steaks, such
    as swordfish or sea bass

salt

4 tsp lemon juice

4 tsp butter

lemon slices, to garnish

method

1 Make 4 baking parchment squares, each large enough to enclose 1 fish steak. Brush the centre of each paper square with a little olive oil.

2 Mix together 1 tablespoon of chopped spring onions with 1 tablespoon of chopped parsley. Spread half over the olive oil, top with 1 fish steak and season to taste with salt. Drizzle over 1 teaspoon of lemon juice, then top with the remaining spring onion and parsley mixture and 1 teaspoon of butter.

3 Bring together 2 sides of the square and make a double fold over the fish. Fold in the ends and tuck underneath the fish, then transfer to a baking sheet. Repeat with the remaining ingredients to make 4 parcels.

4 Brush each parcel lightly with water then bake in a preheated oven, 190°C/375°F/Gas Mark 5, for 20 minutes. Serve the fish in the paper, garnished with lemon slices.

monkfish kebabs

ingredients

SERVES 4

900 g/2 lb monkfish, cut into
    4-cm/1½-inch cubes
freshly cooked rice, to serve

marinade

4 tbsp olive oil
300 ml/10 fl oz plain yogurt
1 tbsp lemon juice
1 medium onion
1 tsp black peppercorns,
    lightly crushed
1 tsp cumin seeds, crushed
salt

method

1 Combine the olive oil, yogurt and lemon juice in a shallow, non-metallic dish. Grate in the onion, then stir in the crushed peppercorns and cumin seeds. Season to taste with salt, then add the monkfish cubes and turn to coat thoroughly in the marinade. Cover and marinate in the refrigerator for at least 2 hours.

2 Divide the monkfish cubes between 4 skewers and cook under a preheated grill for 7–10 minutes until just cooked through, turning frequently and basting with the marinade.

3 Serve immediately on a bed of rice.

baked fish with tomato sauce

ingredients

SERVES 4

4 white fish steaks

salt and pepper

6 tbsp olive oil

2 medium onions, halved
    and sliced

2 garlic cloves, finely chopped

1 celery stalk, chopped

1 carrot, peeled and thinly
    sliced

225 g/8 oz tomatoes, peeled
    and chopped

125 ml/4 fl oz water

lemon wedges (optional) and
    2 tbsp finely chopped
    fresh flat-leaf parsley, to
    garnish

method

1 Season the fish steaks to taste with salt and pepper, then cover and set aside.

2 Heat the oil in a saucepan over medium–low heat. Add the onion, garlic, celery and carrot and cook until the onion has softened. Add the tomatoes and water, season to taste with salt and pepper, and stir to combine. Cover and simmer over low heat for 20 minutes.

3 Spoon a little of the sauce into a baking dish large enough to take the fish steaks in a single layer. Place the fish steaks on top, then pour over the remaining sauce. Bake in a preheated oven, 180°C/350°F/Gas Mark 4, for about 30 minutes, or until the fish flakes easily. Serve immediately or cool to room temperature.

red snapper fillets with lemon cream sauce

ingredients

SERVES 4

1 tbsp butter

1 small onion, chopped

1 garlic clove, crushed

115 g/4 oz mushrooms, sliced

1 tomato, peeled, deseeded
    and diced

1 tbsp tomato paste

salt and pepper

4 red snapper fillets, each
    weighing about 175 g/6 oz

150 ml/5 fl oz water

1 egg yolk

4 tbsp single cream

2 tbsp lemon juice

flat-leaf parsley sprigs, to
    garnish

method

1 Melt the butter in a large frying pan with a lid and cook the onion for 3–4 minutes, until softened but not browned. Add the garlic and cook for a further 30 seconds, then stir in the mushrooms, tomato and tomato paste and season to taste with salt and pepper.

2 Place the fish fillets on top of the vegetables and pour over the water. Bring to the boil, then reduce the heat to medium–low, cover and simmer for 10 minutes, or until the fish is cooked through. Transfer the fish fillets to a serving dish and keep warm.

3 Increase the heat to medium and cook the sauce, stirring, until thick. Whisk together the egg yolk, cream and lemon juice. Gradually add the mixture to the pan, stirring constantly, then remove from the heat and spoon over the fish. Serve immediately, garnished with parsley sprigs.

fish steaks with tomato sauce

ingredients

SERVES 4

2 tbsp olive oil

2 tsp butter

1 large onion, sliced

4 tomatoes, peeled, deseeded
and chopped

2 tbsp tomato paste

225 ml/8 fl oz hot water

4 firm white fish steaks

225 g/8 oz mushrooms, sliced

2 tbsp single cream

salt and pepper

lemon slices and 1 tbsp finely
chopped fresh flat-leaf
parsley, to garnish

method

1 Heat the olive oil and butter in a large frying pan with a lid over medium heat. Add the onion and cook for about 5 minutes, or until softened but not browned.

2 Add the chopped tomatoes, tomato paste and water and stir well. Place the fish steaks in the pan and spoon over the sauce. Cover the pan, reduce the heat to medium–low and simmer for about 10 minutes, turning the fish steaks once. Add the sliced mushrooms to the sauce and cook for a further 3 minutes.

3 Transfer the fish steaks to a warmed serving dish. Stir the cream into the sauce and pour over the fish. Serve garnished with lemon slices and sprinkled with chopped parsley.

sea bass with almond sauce

ingredients

SERVES 4

300 ml/10 fl oz water

salt

6 peppercorns, lightly
    crushed

1 tbsp lemon juice

1 small bay leaf, plus extra
    leaves to garnish (optional)

2 sprigs fresh flat-leaf parsley

4 sea bass fillets, weighing
    about 225 g/8 oz each,
    rinsed and dried

lemon wedges, to serve

almond sauce

4 tbsp fresh white
    breadcrumbs

115 g/4 oz ground almonds

2 garlic cloves

3 tbsp lemon juice

4 tbsp olive oil

salt

method

1 Place the water in a large frying pan with a lid and add salt to taste, the peppercorns, lemon juice, bay leaf and parsley. Bring to the boil and boil for 10 minutes.

2 Carefully add the fish fillets and pour in more boiling water if necessary to cover. Reduce the heat to medium–low, then cover the pan and simmer for 7–8 minutes, or until the fish flakes easily. Allow the fish to cool in the cooking liquid.

3 To make the sauce, place the breadcrumbs, almonds, garlic, lemon juice and 4 tbsp of the cooled cooking liquid in a food processor and process until thick and smooth. With the motor running, add the olive oil in a thin, steady stream. Season to taste with salt and add extra cooking liquid if necessary to make a creamy sauce.

4 Remove the fish from the pan and drain well. Place on individual serving plates, coat with the almond sauce and serve garnished with fresh bay leaves and lemon wedges.

baked sea bass

ingredients

SERVES 4

2 tbsp olive oil

2 tbsp butter

1 onion, thinly sliced

1 carrot, thinly sliced

3 tomatoes, peeled, deseeded
and chopped

1 tbsp tomato paste

55 g/2 oz mushrooms,
thinly sliced

125 ml/4 fl oz white wine

125 ml/4 fl oz water

pinch of paprika

salt

4 sea bass, each weighing
about 275 g/10 oz,
cleaned, rinsed and
patted dry

2 tbsp chopped fresh flat-leaf
parsley, to garnish

method

1 Heat the olive oil and butter in a heavy-based frying pan over medium heat. Add the onion and carrot and cook for 3–4 minutes, until softened but not brown. Add the tomatoes and tomato paste and cook for 5 minutes. Stir in the mushrooms and cook for a further 3 minutes, then stir in the white wine, water, paprika, and salt to taste. Bring to the boil and boil gently until the sauce thickens.

2 Spoon a little of the sauce into a baking dish. Arrange the sea bass on top, then cover with the remaining sauce. Bake in a preheated oven, 190°C/375°F/Gas Mark 5, for 15 minutes. Serve immediately, garnished with chopped parsley.

sea bass in paper

ingredients

SERVES 4

4 sea bass or other white
   fish fillets, weighing about
   225 g/8 oz each
salt and pepper
55 g/2 oz butter, melted
4 tsp lemon
4 bay leaves
4 sprigs fresh thyme
4 sprigs fresh flat-leaf parsley
4 tbsp chopped spring onions
2 large tomatoes, peeled
   and sliced

method

1 Season the fish fillets lightly with salt and pepper and set aside.

2 Make 4 baking parchment rectangles, each large enough to enclose 1 fish fillet. Brush the centre of 1 paper rectangle with a little melted butter. Place a fish fillet on the butter and squeeze over 1 teaspoon of lemon juice. Top with a bay leaf, a sprig each of fresh thyme and parsley, and 1 tablespoon of chopped spring onions.

3 Repeat with the remaining fish fillets. Drizzle a little more butter over the fish fillets and divide the sliced tomatoes between them. Season to taste with salt and pepper and drizzle the remaining butter over the top.

4 Bring together the long sides of 1 paper rectangle and make a triple fold. Double-fold each end and tuck underneath. Transfer to a baking sheet and make the remaining parcels. Sprinkle the parcels with cold water, then bake in a preheated oven, 190°C/375°F/Gas Mark 5, for 25 minutes. Serve immediately, in the paper.

steamed sea bream

ingredients

SERVES 4

4 tbsp butter

350 g/12 oz mushrooms,
    sliced

2 green peppers, sliced

6 tomatoes, peeled, deseeded
    and chopped

salt and pepper

150 ml/5 fl oz white wine

4 tbsp single cream

4 sea bream, each weighing
    about 275 g/10 oz

1 lemon, sliced thinly

2 bay leaves

lemon slices, to serve

method

1 Melt the butter in a large saucepan over medium heat. Add the mushrooms and peppers and cook, stirring, for 4–5 minutes, until softened. Add the tomatoes, season to taste with salt and pepper and cook for a further 3 minutes, stirring constantly. Stir in the wine and cook for a further minute.

2 Remove from the heat and stir in the cream. Arrange the sea bream on top and cover with the lemon slices. Place the bay leaves on top, then cover and cook over medium heat for 20 minutes, or until the fish is cooked through. Serve immediately, garnished with lemon slices.

sardines in vine leaves

ingredients

SERVES 4

24 prepared fresh sardines,
  rinsed and dried
125 ml/4 fl oz olive oil, plus
  extra to serve
salt and pepper
24 preserved vine leaves
juice of ½ lemon
lemon wedges, to garnish
crusty bread, to serve
  (optional)

method

1 Place the sardines in a shallow dish, drizzle over half the olive oil, season to taste with salt and turn the sardines to coat in oil. Cover and marinate in the refrigerator for 30 minutes.

2 Blanch the vine leaves in boiling water for 1 minute, then drain in a colander, rinse well under cold running water, and drain again thoroughly.

3 Remove the sardines from the refrigerator. Place 1 vine leaf, shiny side down, on a work surface and place 1 sardine across the stem end. Sprinkle with a little lemon juice and season with pepper to taste. Fold in the sides of the leaf, then roll it up around the sardine, leaving the sardine head exposed. Repeat with the remaining sardines and vine leaves.

4 Brush the parcels all over with the remaining olive oil and cook under a preheated grill for about 3 minutes on each side, or until the leaves start to scorch. Serve immediately, garnished with lemon wedges, with extra olive oil for drizzling and accompanied with crusty bread, if using.

swordfish stew

ingredients

SERVES 4

125 ml/4 fl oz olive oil

2 medium onions, sliced

2 large waxy potatoes, peeled
and cut into chunks

1 celeriac, peeled and cut
into chunks

4 garlic cloves, very finely
chopped

2 medium tomatoes

salt

900 g/2 lb swordfish, cut into
5-cm/2-inch slices

juice of 1 lemon

1 bunch of fresh flat-leaf
parsley, finely chopped

method

1 Heat half the olive oil in a large saucepan over medium heat. Add the onions and cook for 5 minutes, stirring constantly, until softened but not browned. Pour in 300 ml/10 fl oz of water, stir and simmer for 20 minutes, until the onions have reduced to a purée. Remove from the heat.

2 Place the potatoes, celeriac, garlic and tomatoes in a bowl and mix together. Spread the vegetables over the onions in the pan, season to taste with salt and pour over 250 ml/8 fl oz of water. Cover and cook over medium heat for 20 minutes, or until the potatoes and celeriac are tender.

3 Add the fish to the pan with the remaining olive oil and cook for 15 minutes, or until just cooked through. Gently stir in the lemon juice and parsley, then let the stew cool a little before serving.

white fish stew

ingredients

SERVES 4

4 tbsp olive oil

1 large onion, chopped

2 red chillies, deseeded and
   finely chopped

3 garlic cloves, crushed

2 red peppers, sliced

2 bunches of fresh coriander,
   chopped roughly

450 g/1 lb firm white fish
   fillets, cut into
   5-cm/2-inch chunks

2 tsp dried oregano

salt and pepper

sprigs of fresh coriander,
   to garnish

method

1 Heat the olive oil in a large, heavy-based saucepan. Add the onion and cook over medium heat for about 5 minutes, until softened but not browned.

2 Add the chillies, garlic and peppers and cook, stirring constantly, until the peppers are softened. Stir in the chopped coriander and mix well.

3 Arrange the chunks of fish on top and sprinkle with the oregano and salt and pepper to taste. Cover and cook over low heat for 15–20 minutes, or until the fish is just cooked and flakes easily. Serve immediately, garnished with fresh coriander sprigs.

prawn kebabs

ingredients

SERVES 4

16 large raw prawns, peeled
but tails left on

1 red pepper, cut into
quarters and each quarter
cut into 4 pieces

16 small white mushrooms

1 lemon, cut into 8 chunks

freshly cooked rice, to serve

marinade

4 tbsp olive oil

2 tbsp lemon juice

2 garlic cloves, crushed

½ tsp dried red chilli flakes,
crushed

salt and pepper

method

1 To make the marinade, place the olive oil, lemon juice, garlic and chilli flakes in a shallow, non-metallic dish and season to taste with salt and pepper. Add the prawns and turn to coat in the marinade. Set aside in the refrigerator for 1–2 hours.

2 Divide the prawns, pepper, mushrooms and lemon between 4 skewers and baste with the marinade. Cook under a preheated grill for 5–8 minutes, basting with the marinade and turning frequently, until the prawns are just cooked. Serve immediately on a bed of rice.

anchovies with rice

ingredients

SERVES 4

4 tbsp olive oil

6 tbsp butter, plus extra
    for greasing

1 large onion, chopped

2 tbsp pine nuts

350 g/12 oz long-grain rice

2 tbsp currants

1 tsp allspice

1 tsp cinnamon

salt and pepper

450 g/1 lb fresh or marinated
    fresh anchovies

2 tbsp chopped fresh flat-leaf
    parsley, to garnish

method

1 Heat the olive oil and 4 tablespoons of the butter in a large, heavy-based saucepan. Add the onion and pine nuts and cook over medium–high heat until the onion has softened and turned pale golden. Add the rice, reduce the heat to low and cook, stirring constantly, for 10 minutes.

2 Pour in 750 ml/24 fl oz of water, then add the currants, allspice, cinnamon, and salt and pepper to taste. Bring to the boil, then reduce the heat to medium–low and simmer for 20 minutes, or until the liquid has been absorbed and the rice is tender.

3 Transfer the rice to an ovenproof dish lightly greased with butter and arrange the anchovies on top. Melt the remaining butter and pour over the anchovies. Cover with foil and cook in a preheated oven, 180°C/350°F/Gas Mark 4, for 10–15 minutes, until heated through. Serve garnished with chopped parsley.

stuffed mussels

ingredients

SERVES 6

about 30 large mussels,
    debearded and scrubbed
225 ml/8 fl oz fish stock
lemon slices and fresh parsley
    sprigs, to garnish
hazelnut sauce, to serve
    (see page 156), optional

filling

4 tbsp olive oil
1 onion, finely chopped
2 tbsp pine nuts
85 g/3 oz long-grain rice,
    rinsed and drained
1 tbsp finely chopped fresh
    flat-leaf parsley
115 g/4 oz tomatoes, peeled,
    deseeded and chopped
¼ tsp ground allspice
about 125 ml/4 fl oz hot water
salt and pepper
parsley sprigs, to garnish

method

1 To make the filling, heat the oil in a saucepan, add the onion and cook over low heat for 3–4 minutes, until softened. Stir in the pine nuts and cook for 2 minutes.

2 Add the rice and stir to coat, then stir in the parsley, tomatoes and allspice. Pour in the water and season to taste with salt and pepper. Simmer for about 15 minutes, or until the rice is tender and the liquid has been absorbed, adding more hot water if necessary. Remove from the heat and allow to cool a little.

3 Meanwhile, place the mussels in warm, salted water. As they open, slide the point of a knife between the 2 shells toward the pointed end to sever the closing mechanism. Do not separate the shells, and discard any mussels that do not open.

4 Divide the filling between the mussels. Re-close the shells and tie them up with thin kitchen string to keep them secure. Arrange the mussels in layers in a heavy-based saucepan, then place a plate on top and weight the plate to keep the mussels closed. Add the fish stock, bring to a simmer, then simmer over low heat for 30 minutes. Remove from the heat and cool.

5 Remove the mussels and wipe dry with kitchen paper. Arrange on a serving dish and serve at room temperature or chilled, garnished with lemon slices and fresh parsley sprigs, with hazelnut sauce to accompany, if using.

fried mussels

ingredients

SERVES 6

150 ml/5 fl oz lukewarm water

sugar

1 tsp active dry yeast

175 g/6 oz plain flour

2 tbsp melted butter

salt

2 eggs, separated

about 30 large mussels,
    scrubbed and debearded

150 ml/5 fl oz dry white wine

oil, for deep frying

plain flour, for coating

tahini and walnut sauce, to
    serve (see page 158)

method

1 To make the batter, pour the water into a small bowl, add a pinch of sugar, then add the yeast and stir to dissolve. Set aside in a warm place for about 10 minutes, or until frothy.

2 Sift the flour into a large mixing bowl. Add the melted butter, salt and egg yolks, and mix well. Gradually add the yeast mixture, stirring constantly with a wooden spoon. Cover and set aside in a warm place for about 1 hour.

3 Meanwhile, discard any mussels that are damaged or do not close when tapped sharply. Place the undamaged mussels in a large saucepan with the wine, season lightly with salt, cover the pan and cook over high heat for about 5 minutes, shaking the pan frequently, until the shells open. Remove the mussels from their shells and pat dry on a clean tea towel.

4 Beat the egg whites until stiff, and then fold into the batter. Heat the oil for deep frying in a saucepan until a cube of day-old bread turns brown in 30 seconds. Coat the mussels lightly in flour, then dip them into the batter and immediately drop them into the hot oil. Work in batches to avoid overcrowding the pan. Cook each batch for about 1 minute, or until crisp and golden, then remove with a slotted spoon and drain on kitchen paper. Serve immediately, with tahini and walnut sauce.

vegetarian
& side dishes

One of the best aspects of a cuisine that combines Middle Eastern and Mediterranean traditions is that there is plenty to appeal to those who follow a vegetarian lifestyle. Chickpeas are a favourite ingredient in Turkish cookery and make a satisfying, nutritious and appetizing base for stews – Chickpea Casserole with Spinach and Chickpeas in Spicy Tomato Sauce are just delicious.

Spinach is another key ingredient and works wonderfully well with feta cheese – try Eggs with Spinach for a light lunch or supper dish, or a delectable Spinach Pie, a crisp filo pastry case enclosing a melt-in-the-mouth spinach and feta filling.

Two dishes that appear on every Turkish table to accompany the main course are salad and pilaf. Spinach Salad with Yogurt Dressing and Tomato Salad are both colourful and tasty and can be served with almost anything. There are a few pilaf recipes to choose from here – for a simple accompaniment, go for Orzo Pilaf or Pilaf with Peas, or try Spicy Pilaf or Bulgar Pilaf, packed with vegetables and lightly flavoured with mint, for a more elaborate side dish.

Bread is also served with every meal and it is a joy – and very easy – to make your own fresh Country Bread to mop up sauces, or Pide to scoop up dips or pack with salad. Wonderful!

eggs with spinach

ingredients

SERVES 2

675 g/1lb 8 oz fresh spinach

2 tbsp butter

1 medium onion, finely
    chopped

salt and pepper

55 g/2 oz feta cheese,
    crumbled

4 eggs

method

1 Remove any tough stalks from the spinach, then place it in a colander and rinse well under cold running water. Drain, then shake off any remaining water and shred the spinach.

2 Melt the butter in a medium frying pan with a lid. Add the onion and cook over medium–low heat until softened but not browned. Stir in the spinach and cook, stirring, until the leaves have wilted. Continue to cook until most of the liquid from the spinach has evaporated, then season to taste with salt and pepper and stir in the feta cheese.

3 Press 4 indentations into the spinach with the back of a spoon and break an egg into each. Cover the pan and cook the eggs over medium heat until set. Serve immediately.

spinach pie

ingredients

MAKES 12 SQUARES

2 eggs

3 tbsp olive oil

150 ml/5 fl oz milk

125 ml/4 fl oz water

450 g/1 lb filo pastry

butter, for greasing

filling

1 tbsp olive oil

1 medium onion, finely
  chopped

900 g/2 lb fresh spinach
  leaves, washed and
  shredded

salt and pepper

55 g/2 oz feta cheese,
  crumbled

method

1 To make the filling, heat the olive oil in a large saucepan, add the onion and cook over medium heat for 5 minutes, or until softened but not browned. Add the spinach with the rinsing water clinging to its leaves and cook until the leaves have wilted and all the liquid has evaporated. Season to taste, then stir in the crumbled feta cheese. Set aside.

2 Whisk the eggs, olive oil, milk and water in a bowl. Unwrap the filo pastry and cover with a damp tea towel. Grease a shallow 32 x 22-cm/ 13 x 9-inch baking dish with butter. Place 2 filo sheets in the dish, leaving the edges of the pastry overlapping the sides of the dish. Brush with a little of the egg mixture. Take another 2 filo sheets, fold them in half, and place in the dish. Brush with egg mixture, then continue adding layers of 2 folded filo sheets, brushing each layer with egg mixture, until half the filo sheets have been used.

3 Spread the spinach filling over the pastry, then continue adding layers of 2 folded filo sheets, brushing each layer with the egg mixture, until all the filo sheets have been used. Fold in the overhanging edges of filo pastry and brush the top with the remaining egg mixture. Chill for 2 hours, then bake in a preheated oven, 180°C/350°F/Gas Mark 4, for about 20 minutes, or until crisp and golden brown. Cool, then cut into squares to serve.

stuffed artichokes

ingredients

SERVES 4

8 small globe artichokes

juice of 1 lemon

1 large tomato, cut into
10 slices

filling

150 ml/5 fl oz olive oil

4 medium onions, finely
chopped

1 tbsp pistachio nuts,
chopped

115 g/4 oz long-grain rice,
soaked in warm water for
30 minutes, rinsed and
drained

1 tsp allspice

salt and pepper

2 tbsp finely chopped fresh
flat-leaf parsley

2 tbsp finely chopped fresh
flat-leaf dill

2 tbsp finely chopped fresh
mint

method

1 Snap the stem off 1 artichoke, then peel off the tough outer leaves. Snip off the tough tops of the remaining leaves. Cut off the top 2 cm/ $^3/_4$ inch of the central cone with a sharp knife. Drop the artichoke into a bowl of cold water and lemon juice and prepare the others.

2 Bring 500 ml/16 fl oz of salted water to the boil in a large saucepan, add the artichokes and blanch for 5 minutes. Remove and drain the artichokes, reserving the cooking liquid. Gently separate the artichoke leaves, then remove and discard the central cones. Arrange the artichokes in an ovenproof dish.

3 Heat 4 tablespoons of the oil in a large saucepan and add the onions and pistachio nuts. Cook, stirring, until the onions have softened and the nuts are golden. Add the rice and allspice, season to taste and cook, stirring constantly, for 5 minutes. Add 300 ml/ 10 fl oz of water, cover and simmer for 10–15 minutes, or until the water has been absorbed and the rice is tender. Remove from the heat and stir in the parsley, dill and mint.

4 Divide the filling between the artichokes and wedge the tomato slices around the artichokes. Mix the remaining oil with 150 ml/5 fl oz of the artichoke cooking liquid and pour it into the dish. Bake in a preheated oven, 200°C/400°F/ Gas Mark 6, for 20 minutes. Serve at room temperature.

chickpea casserole with spinach

ingredients

SERVES 4–6

125 ml/4 fl oz olive oil

900 g/2 lb onions, roughly chopped

2 garlic cloves, finely chopped

2 tsp ground coriander

1 tsp ground cumin

1 tbsp paprika

1 bay leaf

450 g/1 lb chickpeas, soaked overnight in cold water and drained

1 litre/35 fl oz cold water

200 g/7 oz potatoes, cut into 2.5 cm/1-inch chunks

200 g/7 oz carrots, cut into 2.5-cm/1-inch chunks

225 g/8 oz fresh spinach, washed, with any thick stalks removed

salt and pepper

method

1 Heat the olive oil in a large, heavy-based saucepan and cook the onions for 5 minutes, or until softened but not browned. Stir in the garlic, coriander, cumin, paprika and bay leaf, then stir in the drained chickpeas.

2 Pour in 750 ml/26 fl oz of water, lay a sheet of baking parchment directly on top of the chickpeas, then cover the pan with a lid. Simmer for 2 hours over very low heat, stirring every half hour.

3 Add the potatoes and carrots, adding more water as necessary, and continue to cook for a further 30 minutes, or until the chickpeas and vegetables are tender. Finally, stir in the spinach and cook until the leaves wilt. If necessary, increase the heat a little to reduce the sauce, then season to taste with salt and pepper. Serve immediately.

chickpeas in spicy tomato sauce

ingredients

SERVES 4

450 g/1 lb chickpeas, soaked
   overnight
3 tbsp olive oil
1 medium onion, finely
   chopped
2 garlic cloves, minced
1 red chilli, finely chopped
115 g/4 oz carrots, finely
   chopped
salt and pepper
300 ml/10 fl oz chicken or
   vegetable stock
400 g/14 oz canned chopped
   tomatoes
1 tbsp tomato purée
1 bay leaf
2 tbsp finely chopped fresh
   coriander, plus extra
   to garnish
freshly cooked rice, to serve

method

1 Drain the chickpeas, place them in a large pan and cover with fresh cold water. Bring to the boil, then reduce the heat and simmer for about 30 minutes, or until tender but still firm. Drain well and set aside.

2 Heat the olive oil in a large, heavy-based saucepan, add the onions, garlic, chilli and carrots, and cook, stirring occasionally, for 5 minutes. Season to taste with salt and pepper, then add the stock, cover and simmer for 15 minutes.

3 Add the chickpeas, tomatoes with their can juices, tomato purée and bay leaf and continue to simmer, covered, for about 1 hour, or until the sauce has thickened. Stir in 2 tablespoons of the chopped coriander, sprinkle with the remaining coriander and serve with rice.

potato casserole

ingredients

SERVES 4

2 strands of saffron

2 tbsp hot water

900 g/2 lb potatoes, peeled

3 tbsp olive oil

350 g/12 oz onions, roughly
  chopped

½ tsp ground coriander

2 tbsp cold water

1 garlic clove, crushed

salt and pepper

1 tbsp chopped fresh flat-leaf
  parsley

1 tbsp chopped fresh
  coriander

method

1 Place the saffron strands in a bowl, cover with the hot water and set aside to infuse.

2 Meanwhile, cut the potatoes into even-sized pieces and place them in a saucepan of lightly salted water. Bring to the boil, then reduce the heat to medium and cook for 10–15 minutes, until tender but still firm. Drain and set aside.

3 Heat 2 tbsp of the olive oil in a large, heavy-based saucepan and fry the onion until softened but not browned. Stir in the ground coriander and cook for a further 2 minutes. Stir in the potatoes, cold water and garlic, and season to taste with salt and pepper.

4 Cover the pan and simmer over low heat, covered, for a further 7–8 minutes. Add the saffron with its soaking liquid and continue to simmer for a further 10 minutes, or until the potatoes are tender and the sauce has thickened.

5 Gently stir in the remaining olive oil with the chopped parsley and coriander and serve.

white bean stew

ingredients

SERVES 4

400 g/14 oz dried cannellini
   beans, soaked overnight in
   cold water and drained
125 ml/4 fl oz olive oil
2 large onions, chopped
2 garlic cloves, chopped
115 g/4 oz carrots, diced
115 g/4 oz celery, diced
4 tbsp tomato purée
½ tsp sugar
pinch of cayenne pepper
juice of ½ lemon
salt
1 tbsp chopped fresh flat-leaf
   parsley

method

1 Place the cannellini beans in a saucepan and cover with cold water. Bring to the boil, then cover the pan and boil gently for 30 minutes. Drain the beans and set aside.

2 Heat the olive oil in a large saucepan, add the onions and cook for 5 minutes, until softened but not browned. Add the garlic, carrots and celery, then stir in the tomato purée, sugar and cayenne pepper. Add the beans and enough water to cover, bring to the boil, then simmer for about 1 hour, or until the beans are tender but still firm and coated in the sauce.

3 Stir in the lemon juice and season to taste with salt. Stir in half the chopped parsley, transfer to a serving bowl, and serve hot or at room temperature, sprinkled with the remaining parsley.

turkish braised vegetables

ingredients

SERVES 4

300 ml/10 fl oz olive oil

1 onion, roughly chopped

2 large carrots, cut into
2.5-cm/1-inch chunks

2 turnips, cut into
2.5-cm/1-inch chunks

1 small celeriac, cut into
2.5-cm/1-inch chunks

1 large potato, cut into
2.5-cm/1-inch chunks

2 leeks, cut into
2.5-cm/1-inch chunks

salt and pepper

juice of 3–4 lemons

large bunch of fresh dill,
finely chopped

method

1 Heat the oil in a large, heavy-based saucepan over low heat. Add the onion and cook, covered, for 5 minutes, stirring occasionally. Add the carrots to the pan and cook, covered, for a further 5 minutes, stirring occasionally. Add the turnips, celeriac and potato to the pan and cook, covered, for a further 15 minutes, stirring occasionally.

2 Add the leeks to the pan and cook, covered, for 5 minutes. The vegetables should be tender but firm.

3 Season to taste with salt and pepper, then add the juice of 3 of the lemons. Taste and add more lemon juice if liked. Serve hot or at room temperature, stirring in the chopped dill just before serving.

chickpea salad

ingredients

SERVES 4–6

450 g/1 lb chickpeas, soaked
     overnight in cold water
     and drained
115 g/4 oz onions, chopped
2 tbsp fresh flat-leaf parsley,
     finely chopped
2 tbsp fresh coriander, finely
     chopped
1 tbsp paprika
1 tbsp cumin
2 garlic cloves, finely chopped
juice of $\frac{1}{2}$ lemon
150 ml/5 fl oz olive oil
450 g/1 lb baby spinach
     leaves
salt and pepper

yogurt sauce

425 ml/15 fl oz Greek-style
     yogurt
2 tbsp fresh coriander,
     chopped
1 garlic clove, very finely
     chopped

method

1 Place the chickpeas in a large saucepan of cold water, bring to the boil, cover and simmer for 1 hour, or until very tender but still firm. Drain, rinse under cold running water and drain thoroughly.

2 Place the chickpeas in a bowl and add the onions, parsley, coriander, paprika, cumin, garlic, most of the lemon juice and 125 ml/4 fl oz of the olive oil. Mix well, then set aside to marinate for 3–4 hours.

3 To make the yogurt sauce, place the yogurt in a serving bowl and stir in the chopped coriander and garlic.

4 Just before serving, toss the spinach leaves in the remaining olive oil and lemon juice and arrange them on a serving plate. Spoon the chickpea salad on top and serve with the yogurt sauce.

spinach salad with yogurt dressing

ingredients

SERVES 4

225 g/8 oz baby spinach
　　leaves, rinsed and drained
¼ small red onion, finely
　　sliced

dressing

4 tbsp Greek-style yogurt
1 tbsp olive oil
1 tbsp lemon juice
1 garlic clove, minced
salt and pepper

method

1 To make the dressing, place all the ingredients in a small bowl and whisk together until thoroughly combined.

2 Pat the spinach leaves dry with kitchen paper and arrange on a serving dish. Add the sliced onion and toss well to combine. Drizzle with the yogurt dressing and serve immediately.

tomato salad

ingredients

SERVES 4

4 medium tomatoes

1 cucumber, peeled

4 tbsp olive oil

3 tbsp lemon juice

1 tsp white wine vinegar

1 tbsp finely chopped fresh
flat-leaf parsley

1 tsp finely chopped fresh
mint

salt and pepper

55 g/2 oz black olives, pitted

method

1 Slice the tomatoes thinly and arrange them in a spiral on a shallow serving dish. Slice the cucumber thinly and arrange the slices between the tomatoes.

2 Whisk together the olive oil, lemon juice, vinegar, herbs and salt and pepper to taste and drizzle over the tomatoes and cucumber. Serve at room temperature, sprinkled with the olives.

spicy pilaf

ingredients

SERVES 6

25 g/1 oz butter

3 tbsp pine nuts

2 tbsp olive oil

85 g/3 oz onion, chopped

400 g/14 oz long-grain rice,
    rinsed and drained

¼ tsp ground cinnamon

pinch of ground allspice

3 tbsp currants

725 ml//24 fl oz chicken stock

salt and pepper

2 tbsp fresh flat-leaf parsley,
    finely chopped

method

1 Heat half the butter in a large saucepan, add the pine nuts and cook, stirring constantly, until golden. Remove using a slotted spoon and drain on kitchen paper.

2 Heat the remaining butter with the olive oil in the same pan, add the onion and cook gently, stirring, until softened but not browned. Add the drained rice and stir to coat the grains. Stir in the cinnamon, allspice and currants, then pour in the chicken stock and season to taste with salt and pepper. Stir once and bring to the boil, then reduce the heat, cover and simmer for 15–20 minutes, or until the liquid has been absorbed and the rice is tender.

3 Remove from the heat, add the pine nuts and chopped parsley and stir gently to combine. Cover the top of the pan with a clean tea towel folded in half, replace the lid and let stand for 15 minutes before serving.

orzo pilaf

ingredients

SERVES 4

3 tbsp orzo

1 tbsp butter

225 g/8 oz long-grain rice

450 ml/16 fl oz hot water

salt and pepper

method

1 Place the orzo in a large, heavy-based saucepan and cook over medium–low heat, stirring constantly, until pale golden brown. Add the butter, rice and hot water to the pan and season to taste with salt and pepper.

2 Stir the rice, bring to the boil, then reduce the heat and simmer, partially covered, over low heat for about 20 minutes, or until the liquid has been absorbed, stirring occasionally when holes start appearing in the rice.

3 Remove from the heat, cover the pan with a clean tea towel folded in half, replace the lid tightly and let stand for 15 minutes before serving.

bulgar pilaf

ingredients

SERVES 4

25 g/1 oz butter

2 tbsp olive oil

1 medium onion, finely
    chopped

1 small green pepper,
    deseeded and chopped

225 g/8 oz bulgar wheat

1 tomato, peeled, deseeded
    and chopped

450 ml/16 fl oz vegetable
    stock

salt and pepper

1 tbsp chopped fresh mint

150 ml/5 fl oz yogurt, to serve

method

1 Heat the butter with the olive oil in a large saucepan over medium heat. Add the onion and cook gently, stirring occasionally, for about 5 minutes, until softened but not browned. Add the pepper and cook for a further 3 minutes. Stir in the bulgar wheat and cook, stirring frequently, for a further 4 minutes.

2 Stir in the tomato and stock and season to taste with salt and pepper. Bring to the boil, stir once, then reduce the heat, cover and simmer for about 20 minutes, or until the liquid has been absorbed and the bulgar wheat is soft. Stir in the mint.

3 Remove the pan from the heat. Cover the pan with a clean tea towel folded in half, replace the lid tightly and let stand for 10 minutes. Fork through the bulgar wheat, then transfer to a serving dish and serve with a bowl of yogurt to accompany.

pilaf with peas

ingredients

SERVES 4

450 ml/16 fl oz water

225 g/8 oz long-grain rice,
    rinsed and drained

2 tbsp olive oil

salt and pepper

115 g/4 oz frozen baby peas

2 tbsp finely chopped fresh
    dill, plus an extra sprig
    to garnish

method

1 Place the water in a saucepan and bring to the boil. Add the rice and olive oil and season to taste with salt and pepper. Reduce the heat, stir the rice once and simmer, covered, for 15–20 minutes, or until the water has been absorbed and the rice is tender.

2 Meanwhile, bring a small saucepan of water to the boil, add the peas and boil gently for 1 minute. Drain thoroughly.

3 Stir the peas and chopped dill into the cooked rice, then cover the pan with a clean tea towel folded in half, replace the lid and let stand for 15 minutes before serving, garnished with the sprig of dill.

hazelnut sauce

ingredients

SERVES 6

150 g/5 oz blanched
    hazelnuts
55 g/2 oz soft white
    breadcrumbs
2 garlic cloves, crushed
1 tbsp water
250 ml/8 fl oz olive oil
125 ml/4 fl oz white wine
    vinegar
1 tsp salt

method

1 Grind the hazelnuts in a food processor, then add the breadcrumbs, garlic and water. With the motor running, slowly add the olive oil in a steady stream.

2 Gradually add the vinegar and process the sauce until smooth, then add the salt. Transfer the sauce to a serving bowl and chill in the refrigerator until required.

tahini & walnut sauce

ingredients

SERVES 6

115 g/4 oz walnut pieces

2 garlic cloves

salt

4 tbsp tahini

juice of 1 large lemon

4 tbsp chopped parsley

method

1 Pound the walnuts, garlic and a little salt together using a pestle and mortar, until the walnuts are broken down but have not formed a paste.

2 Gradually add the tahini and the lemon juice to the walnuts, stirring well to combine. Finally, stir in the chopped parsley and set aside until required.

aubergine sauce

ingredients

SERVES 6

450 g/1 lb small aubergines
1 tbsp lemon juice
55 g/2 oz butter
3 tbsp plain flour
175 ml/6 fl oz milk
55 g/2 oz grated Kashkaval or
    Kasseri cheese
salt and pepper
1 tbsp finely chopped fresh
    flat-leaf parsley, to garnish

method

1 Rinse the aubergines, pat them dry and place them under a grill preheated to the highest setting. Grill the aubergines, turning frequently, until the skins are black and starting to blister and the flesh has softened. Rub the skins off under cold running water, then gently squeeze out as much of the juice as possible. Place the aubergines in a food processor, add the lemon juice and process to a smooth purée.

2 Melt the butter in a heavy-based saucepan and stir in the flour. Cook over low heat for 2 minutes, then gradually add the milk, stirring constantly. Simmer over low heat, stirring, until the the sauce has thickened.

3 Add the aubergine purée to the pan and cook over gentle heat for about 20 minutes, or until the sauce is very thick. Remove the pan from the heat, beat in the cheese, then season to taste with salt and pepper. Serve hot, sprinkled with chopped parsley.

country bread

ingredients

MAKES 1 LOAF

300 ml/10 fl oz water
1 tsp sugar
2 tsp active dry yeast
450 g/1 lb strong white flour
1½ tsp salt
2 tbsp olive oil, plus extra
    for oiling and glazing
1 tbsp poppy seeds

method

1 Place 150 ml/5 fl oz water in a bowl, stir in the sugar, then add the yeast. Set aside for 5 minutes, then whisk.

2 Mix the flour and salt in a large bowl. Make a well in the centre and pour in the yeast liquid. Draw in enough of the flour to form a soft paste, then cover the bowl with a clean tea towel and stand for 20 minutes, until frothy.

3 Pour half of the remaining water and 2 tablespoons of the olive oil into the well, and mix in the flour. Add more water if necessary to form a firm, moist dough. Turn out onto a floured surface and knead for 10 minutes until smooth and elastic.

4 Place the dough in an oiled bowl, turning it to coat in oil. Cover with a clean tea towel and stand in a warm place for 1½–2 hours, until doubled in size. Knock the air out of the dough, then let it stand for 10 minutes.

5 Divide the dough into 3 equal pieces. Roll each piece into a rope shape, then plait the ropes together, pinching the ends to seal. Place on a floured baking sheet, cover with the tea towel and stand for about 45 minutes, until doubled in size.

6 Brush the dough with olive oil and sprinkle with poppy seeds. Bake in a preheated oven, 220°C/425°F/Gas Mark 7, for 40 minutes, or until golden brown and the loaf sounds hollow when tapped underneath. Cool on a wire rack.

pide (pocket bread)

ingredients

MAKES 2 LOAVES

300 ml/10 fl oz water

½ tsp sugar

2 tsp dry yeast

450 g/1 lb strong white flour

1 tsp salt

2 tbsp olive oil

method

1 Pour 100 ml/3½ fl oz of the water into a bowl, stir in the sugar, then sprinkle over the yeast. Set aside for 5 minutes, then whisk.

2 Sift the flour and salt together in a large bowl. Make a well in the centre and pour in the yeast liquid and the olive oil. Mix the flour into the yeast liquid, then add just enough of the remaining water to form a firm, soft dough.

3 Turn the dough out onto a lightly floured work surface and knead for about 10 minutes, until smooth and elastic. Place in a clean, oiled bowl, turning to coat evenly with the oil. Cover with a clean tea towel and stand for about 1½ hours, or until doubled in size. Knock out the air, then stand for 10 minutes.

4 Divide the dough in half and roll each half into a smooth ball. On a lightly floured surface, roll out each piece to form a round 25 cm/10 inches in diameter. Cover with the tea towel and stand for 20 minutes.

5 Transfer the rounds to 2 lightly floured baking sheets. Using a blunt knife, score the top of the loaves 4 times in each direction to make a criss-cross pattern. Bake in a preheated oven, 220°C/425°F/Gas Mark 7 for 10–15 minutes until puffy and golden. Remove from the oven and immediately wrap in clean tea towels to keep the bread soft.

desserts
& cakes

If you have a sweet tooth, then this chapter is pure heaven!

Turkish pastries are well worth mastering – start with Baklava, made from crisp filo pastry with a nut stuffing, topped with a rich syrup flavoured and scented with rose water. Move on to Shredded Pastries with Pistachios, made with a special pastry called kataifi, which is a little more challenging to work with, but very rewarding! After this, you will be ready to tackle the deep-fried pastries which are made, curiously, from a French-style choux-pastry base, demonstrating the European influence on Turkish cuisine.

Milk-based desserts are also popular and appear in many guises – Milk & Almond Dessert, Ottoman Rice Pudding, Chocolate Dessert and Semolina Halva all fall into this category, but bear no resemblance to each other. Noah's Pudding is a festive dish, said to be so-called because it was first made from the leftover food on the last day on the Ark.

Turkish cakes make full use of popular ingredients such as yogurt and citrus fruits, and a particularly delicious confection is Chestnut Dome Cake. If you like a fruity dessert, try Dried Fruit Compote, Apricots Stuffed with Cream or Poached Figs in Rose Water Syrup – none of which are at all virtuous! And of course the one thing you must try is the treat with the name that sums it up perfectly – Turkish Delight.

milk & almond dessert

ingredients

SERVES 6

85 g/3 oz whole blanched
    almonds
900 ml/32 fl oz cold milk
25 g/1 oz ground rice
pinch of salt
4 tbsp sugar
3–4 drops of almond essence
4 tbsp chopped pistachio
    nuts, to garnish

method

1 Grind the almonds finely in a food processor, then transfer to a mixing bowl and knead to make a firm paste.

2 Heat 225 ml/8 fl oz of the cold milk to boiling point, then pour it onto the almond paste and stir until well blended. Set aside to infuse.

3 In a separate large bowl, blend 4 tbsp of the milk with the ground rice. Bring the remaining milk to the boil, then pour it onto the ground rice mixture, stirring constantly. Return the mixture to the saucepan and bring to the boil. Add a pinch of salt, reduce the heat and simmer for 10 minutes, stirring occasionally.

4 Strain the almond milk through a fine sieve into a bowl, pressing the almonds with the back of a spoon. Add the almond milk to the ground rice mixture in the pan, add the sugar and stir well to combine. Simmer gently for a further 10 minutes.

5 Stir in a few drops of almond essence to taste and serve in individual bowls, garnished with chopped pistachio nuts.

ottoman rice pudding

ingredients

SERVES 4

225 g/8 oz short-grain rice

1 litre/35 fl oz milk

250 g/9 oz sugar

1 tsp rose water

method

1 Soak the rice in cold water for 30 minutes, then drain. Place in a heavy-based saucepan with enough water to cover, bring to the boil, then simmer for 5 minutes.

2 Remove the pan from the heat and drain the rice thoroughly. Place the milk in the pan and add the rice. Bring to the boil, stir in the sugar, then reduce the heat and simmer for 10–15 minutes or until the rice is tender. The mixture should be moist and creamy.

3 Remove the pan from the heat, stir in the rose water, then transfer the rice to individual bowls. Set aside to cool, then chill in the refrigerator for 1 hour before serving.

chocolate dessert

ingredients

SERVES 6

125 ml/4 fl oz water

3 tbsp rice flour

1 tbsp cornflour

175 g/6 oz sugar

50 g/1½ oz cocoa powder

1 litre/32 fl oz milk

1 tsp vanilla essence

whipped double cream, to
serve

method

1 Place the water in a heavy-based saucepan, add the rice flour and cornflour and stir to dissolve over medium heat. Add the sugar, cocoa, milk and vanilla essence and cook, stirring constantly, over medium–high heat, until just below boiling point. Reduce the heat to medium and cook, stirring constantly, for a further minute, until smooth and thick.

2 Remove from the heat, cool a little, then divide between 6 individual serving bowls. Cool completely, then chill in the refrigerator. Serve topped with a swirl of whipped cream.

semolina halva

ingredients

SERVES 6

¼ tsp saffron threads
1 tbsp hot water
750 ml/24 fl oz milk
175 g/6 oz sugar
85 g/3 oz unsalted butter
40 g/1½ oz blanched
    almonds, coarsely
    chopped
115 g/4 oz coarse semolina
ground cinnamon, for
    sprinkling

method

1 Pound the saffron threads using a pestle and mortar and transfer to a small bowl. Add the hot water and set aside for 10 minutes.

2 Heat the milk in a heavy-based saucepan. Add the sugar and stir until dissolved, then stir in the saffron water and bring slowly to a gentle boil.

3 Meanwhile, place the butter, almonds and semolina in a heavy-based saucepan over medium–low heat and cook, stirring frequently, for about 10 minutes, or until the almonds are pale golden. Take care not to burn the semolina. Remove the pan from the heat and carefully add the boiling milk syrup.

4 Return to the heat and cook, stirring constantly, until thickened and starting to bubble. Boil gently for 2 minutes, then remove from the heat. Transfer to individual serving dishes and serve at room temperature, sprinkled with cinnamon.

orange water ice

ingredients

SERVES 4

thinly peeled rind of
   2 oranges
thinly peeled rind of 1 lemon
675 ml/24 fl oz water
225 g/8 oz sugar
225 ml/8 fl oz fresh orange
   juice
4 tbsp fresh lemon juice

method

1 Place the orange and lemon rind in a saucepan with the water, bring slowly to the boil and boil, uncovered, for 10 minutes. Strain the liquid into a measuring jug and add more water, if necessary, to make 450 ml/ 16 fl oz.

2 Return the liquid to the pan, add the sugar and cook over medium heat, stirring occasionally, until the sugar has dissolved. Bring to the boil and boil gently, uncovered, for 5 minutes. Remove from the heat and set aside to cool completely.

3 Add the orange and lemon juice to the syrup and stir to combine. Pour the mixture into a shallow, freezerproof container and freeze, uncovered, for about 3 hours, or until firm. Remove from the freezer and break up the water ice with a fork. Serve immediately in chilled glasses.

noah's pudding

ingredients

SERVES 6

55 g/2 oz chickpeas, soaked overnight in water

55 g/2 oz dried haricot beans, soaked overnight in water

140 g/5 oz barley, rinsed and soaked overnight in water

175 g/6 oz sugar

pinch of salt

175 ml/6 fl oz milk

50 g/1¾ oz dried apricots, chopped

50 g/1¾ oz dried figs, chopped

45 g/1½ oz sultanas

45 g/1½ oz currants

2 tbsp blanched almonds, chopped

2 tbsp walnuts, chopped

1 tbsp pine nuts

2 tbsp rose water

pomegranate seeds, to garnish

method

1 Drain the chickpeas and haricot beans, place in separate saucepans, cover with fresh water and cook for 1 hour, or until tender but still firm to the bite.

2 Place the barley with its soaking water in a large, heavy-based saucepan. Add 500 ml/ 16 fl oz of water, bring to a simmer and simmer over low heat, uncovered, for 40–50 minutes, or until very soft.

3 Drain the chickpeas and haricot beans and add to the barley. Stir in 125 ml/4 fl oz of water and cook over low heat, uncovered, for a further 30 minutes, stirring occasionally, until the liquid has evaporated and the mixture is thick.

4 Stir in the sugar, salt and milk and cook for a further 15 minutes. Stir in the apricots, figs, sultanas, currants and nuts, remove the pan from the heat and stir in the rose water.

5 Transfer the mixture to a large serving bowl and allow to cool. Serve at room temperature or cold, garnished with pomegranate seeds.

sultan's turbans

ingredients

MAKES 24

24 filo pastry sheets

175 g/6 oz warm, melted
   unsalted butter, plus extra
   for greasing

syrup

450 g/1 lb sugar

375 ml/12 fl oz water

1 tbsp lemon juice

5-cm/2-inch piece cinnamon
   stick

2 cloves

filling

8 oz/225 g finely chopped
   walnuts

4 tbsp caster sugar

1 tsp ground cinnamon

method

1 To make the syrup, heat the sugar and water in a saucepan over medium heat, stirring to dissolve the sugar. Bring to the boil, add the lemon juice, cinnamon and cloves and boil, without stirring, for 15 minutes. Remove from the heat and strain, discarding the flavourings.

2 To make the filling, combine the ingredients in a bowl and set aside.

3 Place 1 sheet of filo on a work surface with a long edge toward you, covering the remaining sheets with a damp tea towel. Brush the filo sheet lightly with melted butter and sprinkle 2 tablespoons of filling across the lower third, leaving a 3-cm/1¼-inch margin at the bottom and a 1.25-cm/½-inch margin at the sides.

4 Fold the bottom edge of the pastry over the filling and place a 50-cm/20-inch length of 5mm/¼-inch diameter wooden doweling over the folded pastry. Roll the pastry firmly over the doweling and seal the end.

5 Crumple the pastry toward the centre of the doweling until it is less than half its original length, then slide it off. Trim the ends, then roll into a flat coil. Repeat, using the remaining pastry sheets and filling. Place the pastries on a greased baking sheet and bake in a preheated oven, 180°C/350°F/Gas Mark 4, for 25–30 minutes, until crisp and golden. Pour over the syrup and let cool before serving.

baklava

ingredients

MAKES 12 PIECES

375 g/13 oz filo pastry
150 g/5 oz butter, melted
150 g/5 oz walnuts, chopped
150 g/5 oz flaked almonds

syrup

225 g/8 oz sugar
250 ml/8 fl oz water
1 tbsp orange juice
2 tbsp rose water

method

1 To make the syrup, place the sugar and water in a heavy-based saucepan and heat gently, stirring occasionally, until dissolved. Bring to the boil and simmer for about 10 minutes, until a syrup is formed. Remove from the heat, stir in the orange juice and rose water and set aside to cool.

2 Trim the filo pastry sheets to fit a shallow 20 x 30-cm/8 x 12-inch baking pan and cover with a damp tea towel. Grease the pan with a little of the melted butter. Lay 2 sheets of filo loosely in the bottom of the pan and brush lightly with melted butter. Repeat twice.

3 Mix the walnuts and almonds together and scatter half over the pastry. Cover with three more pairs of filo sheets, brushing each pair with melted butter. Scatter over the remaining nuts and cover with three more pairs of filo sheets, brushing each pair with melted butter. Drizzle any remaining butter over the top.

4 Using a large, sharp knife, cut the baklava into 6 squares, then cut each square in half diagonally. Bake in a preheated oven, 180°C/350°F/Gas Mark 4, for about 40 minutes, until golden brown and crisp. Remove from the oven and pour the syrup over the top. Allow to cool completely before serving.

shredded pastries with pistachios

ingredients

MAKES 20

375 g/12 oz kataifi pastry, at
    room temperature
185 ml/6 fl oz warm, melted
    unsalted butter, plus extra
    for greasing
3 tbsp finely chopped
    pistachio nuts, to serve

syrup

250 ml/8 fl oz water
375 g/12 oz sugar
1 tsp lemon juice
3 tsp orange flower water

filling

1 egg white
4 tbsp sugar
175 g/6 oz chopped pistachio
    nuts
150 g/5 oz chopped blanched
    almonds
1 tsp orange flower water

method

1 To make the syrup, stir the water, sugar and lemon juice in a heavy-based saucepan over medium heat until the sugar has dissolved. Bring to the boil and boil for 12 minutes. Stir in the orange flower water, then set aside to cool completely.

2 To make the filling, beat the egg white until stiff. Gradually beat in the sugar, then fold in the nuts and orange flower water.

3 Knead the kataifi pastry in the package to loosen. Take one quarter of the pastry, shape the strands into a 18 x 28-cm /7 x 11-inch rectangle and brush with melted butter. Place one quarter of the filling along one short edge, then roll the pastry firmly into a neat roll. Repeat with the remaining pastry and filling.

4 Transfer the rolls to a rectangular cake pan greased with butter, brush with the remaining butter and bake in a preheated oven, 170°C/325°F/Gas Mark 3, for about 40 minutes, until crisp and golden. Remove from the oven and immediately pour over the cold syrup. Cover with kitchen paper and set aside until the syrup has been absorbed and the rolls are cold.

5 To serve, cut each roll into 5 pieces and sprinkle the top of each pastry with chopped pistachio nuts.

fried dough fingers

ingredients

MAKES ABOUT 20

syrup

225 g/8 oz sugar
375 ml/12 fl oz water
juice of ½ lemon

pastries

150 g/5 oz plain flour
¼ tsp salt
225 ml/8 fl oz water
55 g/2 oz butter
2 large eggs, lightly beaten
almond essence

oil, for shaping and frying
4 tbsp chopped walnuts,
   to serve

method

1 To make the syrup, place the sugar and water in a saucepan and stir over medium heat to dissolve the sugar. Bring to the boil, strain in the lemon juice and boil rapidly, without stirring, for 15 minutes. Remove from the heat and allow to cool.

2 To make the pastry, sift the flour and salt onto a square of baking parchment. Bring the water and butter to the boil, then add the flour all at once, beating constantly with a wooden spoon. Continue beating until the mixture leaves the sides of the pan, then reduce the heat to low and cook for a further 5 minutes.

3 Transfer the mixture to a bowl and cool for 2 minutes. Gradually beat in the eggs, then add a few drops of almond essence and beat until smooth.

4 Transfer the dough to a pastry bag and pipe out 8-cm/3-inch lengths of dough, or make finger-like shapes using oiled hands. Heat oil for deep-frying in a large saucepan to 200°C/400°F, or until a cube of day-old bread browns in 30 seconds. Cook the pastry fingers in batches for 10 minutes, turning frequently, until golden all over. Remove with a slotted spoon and drain on kitchen paper, then turn in the syrup to coat completely and let stand for 5 minutes. Serve warm, sprinkled with chopped walnuts.

sweet borek

ingredients

MAKES ABOUT 20

3 small egg yolks

salt

2 tbsp caster sugar

1 tbsp brandy

2 tbsp yogurt

225 g/8 oz self-raising flour, sifted

oil, for deep-frying

icing sugar, for dusting

method

1 Place the egg yolks in a large mixing bowl, add a pinch of salt and whisk until thick and pale. Beat in the sugar and brandy, then mix in the yogurt. Stir in the flour and mix to a dough, using your hands.

2 Turn the dough out onto a floured work surface and knead until it blisters, then roll out very thinly. Cut the dough into 2.5-cm/1-inch thick strips, then cut each strip into 7.5-cm/3-inch lengths. Tie each strip into a loose knot.

3 Heat the oil for deep-frying over medium heat and cook the pastries, in batches, until puffed and light golden brown, turning once during cooking. Drain well on kitchen paper, then dust with icing sugar and serve warm.

deep-fried pastries with cream & pistachios

ingredients

MAKES ABOUT 24

syrup

225 g/8 oz sugar
375 ml/12 fl oz water
juice of ½ lemon

pastries

150 g/5 oz plain flour
¼ tsp salt
225 ml/8 fl oz water
55 g/2 oz butter
2 large eggs, lightly beaten
almond essence

oil, for shaping and frying
300 ml/10 fl oz double cream,
   whipped
4 tbsp finely chopped
   pistachio nuts, to serve

method

1 To make the syrup, place the sugar and water in a saucepan and stir over medium heat to dissolve the sugar. Bring to the boil, strain in the lemon juice and boil rapidly, without stirring, for 15 minutes, then cool.

2 Make the pastry, following the method in Steps 2 and 3 on page 186.

3 Using oiled hands, make walnut-sized balls of dough and place on an oiled baking sheet. Flatten each ball into a 5-cm/2-in round and make a hole in the centre with an oiled finger.

4 Heat 1.25 cm/½ inch oil in a large, heavy-based frying pan until just warm. Add half the pastries, increase the heat to medium–high and cook for 15 minutes, turning frequently, until the pastries are well risen and golden all over. Remove, drain on kitchen paper and cook the second batch.

5 Turn the pastries in the syrup to coat, then let stand for 5 minutes. Transfer to a serving dish, place a little whipped cream in the centre of each and serve sprinkled with pistachio nuts.

dried fruit compote

ingredients

SERVES 4

115 g/4 oz prunes, pitted

115 g/4 oz dried apricots

115 g/4 oz sultanas

55 g/2 oz sugar

thin strip of lemon rind

2 cloves

5-cm/2-inch piece cinnamon
  stick

2 tbsp chopped walnuts,
  to serve

method

1 Rinse the prunes, apricots and sultanas under cold running water and place in a large saucepan. Cover with cold water, bring to the boil, then cover and simmer over low heat for 15 minutes.

2 Add the sugar and stir until dissolved, then add the lemon rind, cloves, cinnamon stick and a little more water if necessary. Simmer over low heat, uncovered, until the fruit is tender but still firm and the syrup is thick. Remove from the heat and remove and discard the lemon rind, cloves and cinnamon.

3 Transfer to a bowl, cool, then chill completely in the refrigerator. Sprinkle with walnuts to serve.

caramelized butternut squash

ingredients

SERVES 4

450 g/1 lb butternut squash, cut into 2.5-cm/1-inch chunks

115 g/4 oz sugar

2 tbsp water

pinch of cinnamon

4 tbsp pistachio nuts, lightly crushed

method

1 Place the butternut squash, sugar, water and cinnamon in a large saucepan. Cook over medium–low heat, uncovered, stirring occasionally, for about 30 minutes, or until the water has evaporated and the squash is tender and caramelized. Add a little more water if necessary to prevent the squash sticking to the pan.

2 Transfer to a serving dish and cool, then serve sprinkled with crushed pistachio nuts.

apricots stuffed with cream

ingredients

SERVES 4

175 g/6 oz whole dried
    apricots
375 ml/12 fl oz water
thin strip of lemon rind
115 g/4 oz sugar
1 tsp lemon juice
175 ml/6 fl oz double cream
    or Mascarpone
2 tbsp finely chopped
    pistachio nuts, to serve

method

1 Soak the apricots overnight in cold water, then drain. Place the water, lemon rind and sugar in a saucepan. Cover the pan and bring slowly to the boil, then boil over medium–high heat for 10 minutes. Add the apricots and simmer over low heat for 10 minutes, or until tender. Remove the pan from the heat, stir in the lemon juice and set aside to cool.

2 Using a slotted spoon, transfer the cooled apricots to a sieve, letting the excess syrup drip back into the pan. Return the pan to the heat, bring the syrup to the boil and boil for 1 minute, until reduced. Strain the syrup into a jug, cool completely, then chill in the refrigerator until required.

3 Whip the double cream, if using. Gently squeeze each apricot open and insert 1 teaspoon of whipped cream or Mascarpone. Arrange the apricots on a serving dish in a single layer, cover and chill.

4 To serve, pour the cold syrup over the apricots and sprinkle with the chopped pistachio nuts.

poached figs in rose water syrup

ingredients

SERVES 4

250 g/9 oz caster sugar

grated rind and juice of
   1 orange

6 cardamom pods, lightly
   crushed

8 fresh figs

½ tsp rose water

225 g/8 oz Greek-style yogurt

method

1 Place the sugar, orange rind and juice, cardamom pods and 300 ml/10 fl oz of cold water in a heavy-based saucepan. Stir over medium heat until the sugar has dissolved, then bring to the boil.

2 Add the figs to the syrup and reduce the heat to low. Cover the figs and syrup tightly with a sheet of baking parchment, then simmer for 8–10 minutes, until the figs start to soften.

3 Remove the figs from the pan with a slotted spoon and set aside in a serving bowl. Simmer the syrup for a further 7–8 minutes, or until slightly reduced, then stir in the rose water.

4 Pour the syrup over the figs and cool slightly before serving with yogurt.

turkish delight

ingredients

MAKES 81 SQUARES

1 kg/2 lb 4 oz granulated
    sugar
1.1 litres/36 fl oz cold water
1 tsp lemon juice
150 g/5 oz cornflour
1 tsp cream of tartar
2 tbsp rose water
red food colouring
sunflower oil, for brushing
85 g/3 oz icing sugar

method

1 Place the sugar, 375 ml/12 fl oz of the water and the lemon juice in a large, heavy-based saucepan over low heat. Stir until the sugar dissolves, bring to the boil and boil until the mixture reaches 115°C/240°F on a sugar thermometer. Remove the pan from the heat.

2 Blend 115 g/4 oz of the cornflour, the cream of tartar and 250 ml/8 fl oz of the water in a large heatproof bowl until smooth. Bring the remaining water to the boil in a large, heavy-based saucepan and stir it into the cornflour mixture in the bowl. Return the mixture to the pan, place over medium heat and cook, whisking constantly with a balloon whisk, until the mixture thickens and bubbles.

3 Gradually add the hot syrup, stirring constantly. Bring to the boil and boil gently, stirring regularly with a wooden spoon, for about 1¼ hours, or until the mixture is pale golden. Stir in the rose water and enough red food colouring to tint the mixture pale pink. Pour into a 23-cm/9-inch square cake pan lightly brushed with oil and set aside for 12 hours.

4 Combine the icing sugar and the remaining cornflour in a shallow dish. Cut the Turkish delight into 2.5-cm/1-inch squares using an oiled knife and toss in the sugar mixture. Store in a sealed container with the remaining sugar mixture sprinkled over.

yogurt cake

ingredients

SERVES 6–8

4 large eggs, separated

115 g/4 oz caster sugar

3 tbsp plain flour

400 g/14 oz Greek-style
    yogurt

finely grated rind of 1 lemon

butter, for greasing

syrup

150 ml/5 fl oz water

250 g/9 oz caster sugar

juice of 1 lemon

finely grated rind of 1 orange

method

1 Beat the egg yolks and sugar until thick and pale. Beat in the flour, then beat in the yogurt and lemon rind until thoroughly combined.

2 Whisk the egg whites until stiff and fold them lightly into the yogurt mixture. Turn the mixture into a greased 23-cm/9-inch round baking pan lined with baking parchment. Bake in a preheated oven, 180°C/350°F/ Gas Mark 4, for about 1 hour, or until golden brown – the cake will rise and then collapse.

3 Meanwhile, to make the syrup, boil the water with the sugar, lemon juice and orange rind for 5 minutes. Cool completely, then chill in the refrigerator.

4 Remove the cake from the oven and cool slightly in the pan, then turn out onto a serving plate. Serve warm, with the syrup.

chestnut dome cake

ingredients

SERVES 8

900 g/2 lb canned whole
    chestnuts
225 g/8 oz icing sugar
1 egg yolk
4 tbsp unsalted butter
2 tbsp cocoa
200 g/7 oz tea biscuits
125 ml/4 fl oz warm milk
grated chocolate, to decorate
whipped double cream,
    to serve

icing

6 tbsp butter
175 g/6 oz icing sugar
3 tbsp cocoa powder
1 tsp vanilla essence
2–3 tbsp milk

method

1 Place the chestnuts in a food processor and chop finely. Add the sugar, egg yolk, butter and cocoa and process to a purée.

2 One at a time, soak about two-thirds of the tea biscuits briefly in the milk and use to line the bottom and sides of a 1.5 litre/48 fl oz dome-shaped mixing bowl. Fill the bowl with the chestnut mixture, then soak the remaining biscuits and use to cover the filling. Cover with clingfilm and chill in the refrigerator overnight.

3 To make the icing, beat the butter in a bowl until soft. Beat in the sugar and cocoa with the vanilla essence and enough milk to make a smooth spreading consistency.

4 To serve, loosen the cake with a round-bladed knife and turn out onto a serving plate. Coat the cake with the icing, sprinkle with grated chocolate and serve with a spoonful of whipped cream.

lemon syrup cake

ingredients

MAKES 9 SQUARES

115 g/4 oz flour

1 tbsp baking powder

115 g/4 oz semolina

115 g/4 oz sugar

1 tbsp olive oil

1 tsp vanilla essence

4 eggs

butter, for greasing

whipped double cream and
    chopped pistachio nuts,
    to serve

syrup

250 ml/8 fl oz water

115 g/4 oz sugar

1 tbsp lemon juice

method

1 Sift the flour and baking powder into a bowl and stir in the semolina.

2 Whisk together the sugar, olive oil, vanilla essence and eggs, then beat the mixture thoroughly into the flour and semolina. Transfer to a 20-cm/8-inch square shallow cake pan lightly greased with butter and bake in a preheated oven, 190°C/375°F/Gas Mark 5, for 25 minutes, until well risen and golden.

3 Meanwhile, make the syrup. Place the water, sugar and lemon juice in a saucepan, bring to the boil and boil for 5 minutes. Remove from the heat and cool slightly.

4 Remove the cake from the oven and immediately pour over the warm syrup. Cool completely, then serve cut into squares, with whipped cream and a sprinkling of chopped pistachio nuts.